Queen-ish:

The Tilted Crown of Womanhood

WORDS MATTER
PUBLISHING
OUR WORDS CHANGE THE WORLD

ISBN: 978-1-953912-72-5

Library of Congress Catalog Card Number: 2022938408

Acknowledgements

This book taught me to create stability even if the ground beneath you isn't stable—I lost my job during the pandemic, lost dear family members to cancers and heart issues, got pregnant, and had a baby all while writing this book. It was an outlet to escape reality at some points. I had so much fun with it but I will admit it wasn't a walk in the park or a piece of cake and there were days I lacked motivation. From tears of frustration, throwing up from a growing uterus, losing loved ones, and adjusting to being a different kind of wife and mom it was still worth it. However, It wasn't all me—not even close.

I couldn't have done it without the following people and inspirations: I thank life and all the women in my life, for being so full of lessons and God for allowing me to be smart enough and attentive enough to realize those lessons. All the quoted authors from each chapter, I admire your work and your knowledge. You helped put into better and shorter words what I was trying to say. I'd like to thank all the friends who contributed their real stories, who I won't mention by name out of respect for their privacy. They humbled themselves all for me to make a point and show others we aren't as alone as we think we are. I'd like to thank my family for always inspiring me to reach for the sky and reach for the limit no matter what's going on in my life. Specifically, my new baby daughter (who made what I said in the book really matter), my mom, husband, and uncles who are no longer with us. They reminded me that life worked on its own timeline, that I had the talent to use it and not sit on it, and that it was okay to get overwhelmed by wanting to be great. You are missed and I love you forever dear uncles. I'd like to specifically call out the people who unexpectedly became a huge source of confidence, faith, and guidance - those at Words Matter Publishing. Especially Tammy Koelling and Steve Wilson. You guys believed in me, spent the hours it took to get this book where it is today and gave me a home in the book world. You reminded me that I had a team at my toughest points. You truly had my back and kept me on course. And most of all, I thank my readers for picking up this book, for wanting to make a change, and for seeing the vision. It was all up to you anyway. I prayed that God allowed me to be a bridge that led you to the woman you are supposed to be. God bless you all!

Table Of Content

Introduction

Excuse me, ladies! It is time we have a serious conversation. A conversation that has been needed for some time now. A conversation you cannot just walk away from. It appears to me that we have forgotten something important. What is it, you ask? That we are royalty! We are the leaders of the world. We are Mother Nature. We. Are. Women. Women are divine beings. So, why are we not acting like it?

This is girl-talk in a book. Except, I am not going to sugarcoat anything! I'm not going to beat around the bush with you. This is the kick in the pants you never knew you needed. That is why you picked up this book, isn't it? I am going to tell it like it is. I am using my own embarrassing stories, common sense, hardlearned lessons, and some living examples too. I am like that big sister or that friend you call when you want to know the truth. Because I have no reason to lie to you. We can all learn from each other so grab some wine, get with your friends and let's talk!

I find it odd that women of all ages, but mostly my generation, don't know how powerful and amazing they truly are. We seek permission to be great, we second-guess ourselves, and I want to talk about why we do those things and how we should stop them...Like yesterday!

It will not be easy or even comfortable for that matter. But it is worth it and it is up to you to put the leg work in. Revamping our mindset, snatching our confidence and our lives back will take some serious effort. Starting with realizing the issues we are causing for ourselves, our children, and other women in the world in this day and age. Today's problems are totally different than what they were fifty or even ten years ago. We have issues and new things happening that we need to be better prepared for.

What—do you think you are the only lady who has made yourself sick with your diet, crying yourself to sleep after a bad breakup, putting a man over your children, over God? Ha. Think again. These are common issues in womanhood, but that should not make them acceptable. Whatever it is that you do when you are a woman facing a crisis in your life...I am sure there is another out there doing the same thing. Hey, it might be another lady who picked up this book. But I think it's me and I think you've met your match.

Our very mistakes are what tie us together. Commonality: If you talk to your girlfriends about your issues, they probably say, "*Girl, I remember when that happened to me.*" The only thing that sets us apart as women is the way we respond to these issues. Some women curl up in a ball, cry, and then make the same mistakes again and again. Then ask why this keeps happening to them. They throw a pity party. Others ball up, cry, and reflect...coming back smarter and stronger. They make the decision to not make the same mistake because they remember how it felt. So scratch that b.s. about the older you get, the wiser you get. Wisdom is not an automatic skill acquired with age. Being wiser is a choice. I know plenty of adults and elders who are as smart as a bag of rocks. Do you want to learn from your mistakes or not? Do you want to be a better woman? That's what makes you different from your neighbor.

However, how will we ever snap back if we are too busy weeping and feeling sorry for ourselves when ordinary things do happen? Or when we are comparing ourselves to women that we find respectable and beautiful. We spend so much time worried and chasing the wrong things that we do not see the truth for what it is—natural. Who cares if your friend got engaged and you did not? We do. Who cares if she got the shoes you wanted two weeks ago at that mall? *I mean why would she buy those shoes if I told her that I liked them? Guess what's next? She will be trying to take my man too.* Since we were all young girls, we dreamed of Prince Charming and having our own fairytales. Now we are ruining fairytales. We are portraying negative behavior for other women to mimic: like our daughters, the next generation of women in the world.

And what is up with that? Why do we disrupt other women's dreams for our own happiness? We all want to be happy, but our happiness shouldn't be at the expense of others. We should let others be happy and decide to be happy with ourselves. I have been through so much in this one lifetime but I told myself that I choose to be wise and happy. Because I'm a mother-freaking Queen. Duh. I believe in God, and I believe in using a good ole curse word from time to time too. However, for the sake of your kid picking this book up, I'm going to replace curse words with ridiculously funny words. Like what I just did. So don't judge me and I won't judge you. I'm just a straight-up person and I am who I am.

I wrote this book to reassure you that you are not worthless, stupid, or going to die alone. You are a Queen. You just happened to lose your way. You just happened to let your crown get crooked. We are all Queens, maybe of different things, but that does not make us any less than the next. There is a man out there for you, but you have to be ready. Sorry sista, but you are not ready until you have healed those wounds, and you know how to love yourself more than anyone else - until you are comfortable with your own company, until you have become the woman you want to be without your man's help! That a man cannot do, he cannot teach you how to love yourself more than he loves you. The only man I know who can do that is God.

The problems of this decade are not the same as the last decade, and the 20th century definitely comes with difficulties unique to its own era. From social media to the new expectations of society to questions about sexuality, we live in a confusing world, and the times have only gotten worse for women. Women cannot even make personal decisions for their bodies without it becoming a political debate. Face it, we just have problems that men do not. We even have problems that my grandmother did not.

A new era brings new problems. So first of all, we need to come up with a *new* way to deal with our *new* issues of today. Chivalry is dead. Men are operating in their own world, they are not worried about us. *We* have to have our own backs. To do that we need to stop tolerating disrespect from them, other women, and definitely ourselves…it is all up to us at the end of the day. We are the mothers, daughters, sisters, and wives of today and must lay some ground for tomorrow. So, let us claim it and stop having our pity party now. Pity for the woman is dead.

Trust me, you will be reflecting on this book again, and I strongly urge you to. So grab your highlighters and pens because this book has empty pages for your stories too. Find them at the end of each chapter, when you are asked a series of questions from the reading. Ready? Let's go!

Why did you pick up this book?
The Checklist:

- You've put everyone in your life first and need to do something for you
- Your emotions control your life
- You want to make a change in your life
- You want to hear other women's embarrassing stories to feel better about yourself
- You're wondering why you can't keep friends or a man
- You've forgotten your woman power and who you are
- You wanted to read something fun
- You keep comparing yourself to other women
- Forget it…mark ALL THE ABOVE!

CHAPTER 1

There's No Such Thing as Perfect

Perfection—a word with a loaded meaning in today's world, especially in womanhood. It's a word that's often overused or used irresponsibly. This is pressure, an expectation, or a bad habit of present-day society often affecting women so strongly that they end up with depression, anxiety, insecurity, self-scrutiny, and even imposter syndrome. We end up hating ourselves and sabotaging our uniqueness. Perfectionism is a word taking over everywhere in our lives, but most especially in appearance and body image. We all strive to be the perfect woman. She has the perfect body. She is the perfect wife, president, or CEO at work and the best mom in the world. She laughs cute, doesn't argue and she is so perfect that a person would question if she even farts or ever messes up. We are always yearning or reaching for that perfect life. We are always farting. Or at least I am. It's whatever.

We live in a wanna-be fairytale where we have to strive for perfection in everything as if we were robots. Which is ridiculous because no one can be a master of all trades. No one can actually be perfect. You will mess up somewhere because you're human. The ideal life is just not realistic. To me, that just

1

sounds like a made-up woman in a made-up life somewhere in a made-up world. I am far from perfect. I don't have big boobs, I yell when I am arguing sometimes, sneeze a bit too loud, and burst out and snort with laughter at the

~~

"Matthew 19:21: Jesus told him, "If you want to be perfect, go and sell all your possessions and give the money to the poor, and you will have treasure in heaven. Then come, follow me."

~~

worst times. I am not perfect and I accept it. It is what it is.

However, two particular categories go hand-in-hand that women try to be perfect in...Possessions and appearance. Women often strive for perfection in superficial things such as accessories, boobs, cars, and makeup. We judge a woman's character by the way she carries herself, by her makeup, her hair, her car, and her nails. You know all the things that tell you nothing about the woman's character. Did it ever occur to you that we are more than looks? We are more than our appearance and have nothing to be insecure about.

I hate to break it to you ladies, there's no such thing as perfect. Nothing can be perfect no matter where you try to achieve it in your life.

~~

"Let's just try to be real instead of perfect."

~~

So just stop trying. Sorry sis, but I'm keeping it real. Part of obsessing with perfection is never being satisfied with what you have. Be grateful. Everything cannot be perfect. To be perfect is to be without error and that is simply impossible. It's okay to make mistakes, you learn from them. Just don't make the same ones again and again. Make new mistakes! The last area where we should be trying to be perfect is in terms of physical things or belongings. If we are going to aim for any sort of perfection let it be in who we are as a person. Or just simply our best version, that can't even be perfect.

Can we just not use the word perfect anymore? We can replace it with better. We only get better, not perfect. Let's be our beautifully imperfect selves. Accept the fact that you will mess up, you will have a bad hair day, hairy legs and armpits, and that you do have flaws in your personality. God has accepted that! After all, He is the one who gave all of this to us. He gave us the chance to better ourselves with free will, the book of knowledge, and the armpit hair. What He won't accept is you being a crappy person. We are spending all this time and money getting things sucked, tucked, lifted, and shifted trying to look and live like the ladies on TV and in magazines who are making the same mistakes. We sometimes even put ourselves in pain to

~~

"Whenever you feel unloved, unimportant, or insecure, remember to whom you belong."
- Ephesians 2:19-22

~~

3

look like these people. What a stupid cycle! Let's just try to be real instead of perfect. Let's just try our best and that's it. Why do we look for perfection and acceptance in our physical attributes? Because we gullibly think it is a result we can achieve.

We don't know the truth behind the scenes of how that woman in the commercial looks like that. Liposuction, plastic surgery, video editing tricks, the gym? Who knows and who cares? We do. We always do.

We try to be perfect and look perfect, but remember there is no such thing. It is nothing but a fantasy. We often hurt ourselves and others to complete this impossible mission of perfection. God kept it real from the beginning. He said we are all born with sin, even those ladies on TV and billboards. He also said in the Bible that we should stop focusing on material or superficial things because that isn't what makes us worthy in His eyes. Your car, house, or body shape may be nice but they aren't going to get

~~

"Do not let your adorning be external—the braiding of hair and the putting on of gold jewelry, or the clothing you wear— but let your adorning be the hidden person of the heart with the imperishable beauty of a gentle and quiet spirit, which in God's sight is very precious."
- 1 Corinthians 6:19-20

~~

you into heaven. Do you know what helps me not idolize the celebrities and mentally embody them as the symbol of perfection? I remind myself that every single one of these so-called perfect ladies has failed at something, been insecure about something,

~~

"You are beautiful. For you are fearfully and wonderfully made..."
- Psalms 139:14

~~

and had diarrhea just like me. All of them have made terrible decisions before. All of them are people just like you and me. That makes me feel better. Get them off the pedestal and stop idolizing other people because of their worldly possessions or appearance. That is so fake.

Let's not forget that everything we see or sell is on purpose. We forget that our insecurities are the one-way street into our pockets, making mainstream cosmetic companies so rich it stinks. Unfortunately, companies are eating it up. This energy, this elephant in the room, has become a part of the way women think and feel about themselves. It's devastating that we are believing we need all these things to be perfect as if it's actually attainable in the first place. It's a joke.

The lie that we have to be perfect is the way of the world and what it pressures us to be. It is the way of the world to get us wrapped in its chaos and make us buy into that. Frankly, if we are going to spend time making anything as close to perfect as possible, let it be our soul, who we are at our core. All the perfect things we try to be are materialistic and superficial. Just like all of the "perfect-looking" superstars posing on billboards, social media, and reality t.v. Their photoshopped, plastic-filled, airbrushed faces are everywhere and if you don't look or live like them then you are made to believe you aren't a beautiful woman. You are being way too hard on yourself girl, that's bullcrap. If you aren't perfect, that doesn't mean you aren't worth it.

It seems like people of my generation want to be "thick". At least, thick in all the "right" places. And let me explain, there's been this silent shift to being perfect if you are a thick-lipped, thick-boobed, thick-bottomed woman. While you have to be this thick lady there is this absurd expectation that you'll have a tiny waist too. I think this is impossible unless you're an anime cartoon. We have simply forgotten that big butts and big boobs likely come with a big waist too and that there is nothing wrong with that. That's why we are wearing shapers, veneers, starving ourselves, or in my past, overeating to gain the things that we assume men are supposedly looking for now. If that is the type of man you date you need to choose better qualities. If they hold these expectations of perfection, they don't matter and you don't need that in your life.

Most men don't obsess over perfection or spend nearly as much on surgeries and shapers for their looks as women do, and I feel like they are much happier people because of that. Men are attracted to women of all shapes, colors, and sizes. They aren't asking for one type of woman. How boring would that be if all of us looked the same? Real men, at least the decent ones, aren't asking for perfection from us...they know we're human. You know, there are some men who would pay for your boobs to look perfect and pay for anything to make you seem perfect because they are chasing their infatuation with having a trophy wife. There are men who settle for those superficial, exhausting, pointless highs of perfection. However, I think they exist because women have allowed them to. We push so hard for perfection, so men feel like it's okay to demand it. It's not even cultural because I see these types of people everywhere and in a variety of ages. But what I think it is…it's women that assume all men want us to be perfect. I mean these are the women they look at when we aren't around right? Isn't this what they all want? eh…I think most men just want a *real* woman. The same way most of us want a *real* man. Men just want someone to treat them like the big baby they are when they are sick, for god's sake. Most couldn't care less about a designer purse, latest make-up trends, plastic surgery, expensive creams, and push-up bras. Some of them don't even notice when you use these things so you might as well stop chasing them like a fiend.

You mean to tell me…all the men of the world got together at some secret meeting women didn't know about to discuss how they wanted *only* big-bottomed and tiny-waisted women? Absurd. It's laughable, but it's so sad because God cares nothing about these things! So if someone doesn't love us for how we look and God does, who cares what they think! Love you for you!

I'm going to share something personal with you because I believe through sharing my story, that you'll better understand yours. I was always careful to maintain a public impression that I was confident and thought I was hot spit, but every woman has insecurity behind closed doors (generally speaking). Before I found self-love in all things physical, I used to stuff myself. Yeah, you read that right. When I was in elementary school I would ball up toilet paper and put it in my training bras. While all the girls in my classes were growing little boobies and wearing real bras, I was still in training bras and wanted my "mosquito bites" to grow like theirs very badly. My mom wasn't too happy when she caught me but she understood. One day she just walked right up to me and squeezed my chest.

She asked why my chest felt so hard and looked so unproportioned and stiff. We went into the room to discuss what was going on from one woman to another. She put her hand down my shirt and reached right into my bra and snatched the toilet paper out! She caught me red-handed. "Why are you doing this?" she asked. "You need to stop now.".

"Ma, I want boobs like the other girls," I replied. She proceeded to tell me that I'd get boobs when it's time for me to get them and that some people can be pretty and have big boobs but have big personality issues along with that. She told me I had a big personality and more going for my life than big boobs. She concluded by telling me to stop wasting her money by stuffing myself with toilet paper. I didn't, I just stuffed them less so she wouldn't assume I was still doing it. I stopped somewhere around fifth grade. It took me until my freshman year in college to accept me for me and strive for my best regarding my personality.

Up until then, that mentality never fully went away, the difference is that I don't have to stuff myself cause now there are push-up bras that add cup sizes. Even in high school I found myself looking at other girls' thick body shapes and wanting to be shaped the same way. I failed to realize that I was slim and trim because I was going to be a national contending track and field collegiate athlete. My body was meant to be toned and defined for explosive sprinting, not big-booty-Judy like the rap videos I watched in my pre-teens on MTV. I had a different purpose than the women I treasured because of their appearance. My body was designed for my purpose. I found my way to flip it, or you know, look on the bright side.

That's when I prayed and read the Bible and realized that God does not judge me by materialistic or physical standards. He doesn't care about my nails, hair, jewelry, or all the things the world tells us to care about. I found love for who I am. Now, I know I am an awesome sexy chocolate goddess inside and out. Now you won't catch me stuffing myself or wearing push-up bras every day because I love my chocolate cups (boobs). So I need you to get to the point where you feel that way about yourself! And the only way that'll happen is by changing your perception.

Your inner values and who you are cannot be determined by your features or belongings. I don't think God will judge you by the size of your derriere or your boobs. God loves you for who you are on the inside, not for how appealing you are on the outside. You have got to start thinking about what you bring to the table! You are the blasted table...so wake up!

You may have similar insecurities but try to think of your God-given purpose. Perfection isn't what gets you into Heaven.

God turned away so many people in the Bible who were seen as perfect on the outside. Think about it, Jesus died for us when we were sinners. He thought we were that worthy. So ladies, we need to stop treasuring the worldly things so much.

This drive to be perfect says nothing about your personality. How many times have we seen the prettiest, most perfect girl in the room be the meanest, most selfish, or the loneliest? Personality and inner qualities are the things we should be powering up, spending money on, lifting and shifting. It's time for us to stop running away from that. If you are going to focus on upgrades, focus on spiritual ones—focus on making your personality better or getting closer to the man who already loves you as is—God! Why don't we love ourselves similarly? Sis, you need to take a step back and re-evaluate yourself. I think that's what we need to do as a whole. Now more than ever.

Where have you aimed for perfection that you shouldn't have? When have you forgotten that inner qualities matter most? How can you change the way you see perfection?

_____

_____

_____

_____

_____

_____

_____

_____

_____

_____

_____

_____

_____

_____

_____

_____

_____

_____

CHAPTER 2

Compare, Camouflage, and Compete

This chapter and chapter one go hand-in-hand, that's why they come one after another. Honey, these three C's are the worst things you could do to yourself as a woman! However, I see women bringing themselves down by allowing competition and comparisons to take away their uniqueness and the best parts of their lives. These three C's inhabit

"Exodus 20:17: You shall not covet your neighbor's house, you shall not covet your neighbor's wife, or his male servant, or his female servant, or his ox, or his donkey, or anything that is your neighbor's."

~~

traits that make you jealous, make you a bully, ruin your self-esteem, and ruin friendships and relationships.

Women compare themselves to others almost every day! From seven years old through adulthood, we find ourselves measuring who we are and our lives with others. I noticed from a young age that if you aren't in first place you definitely have to compete for it. It's just a thing. I know it's always been a problem but I didn't do anything about it until I got older. We could even get scientific about it and say it's in our nature to compete. Women play copy-cat by adapting to what others are doing. Once that happens, we compete by trying to be better than the others. Some women supposedly "thrive" in this nasty, competitive environment and start to put other women down while others do horribly and find themselves being trampled over. The truth is we all fail when we do this. No one is thriving, we only become hypocritical, judgmental, crude individuals. Why do we compare and compete all the time? We want to be prized. Why do we camouflage ourselves when we notice we are different from others? Because we want to be in the running for the "prize." See the cycle? Most women compare, camouflage, and compete because they feel they have no choice as others around them are doing it. Some do it in hopes of feeling better about themselves. That's when it gets detrimental. I have been all of the above as a college athlete, a student, a coworker, a friend, and a significant other. I found myself being a winner and a loser at different points and subject to these three C's too. Then I decided a few years ago that I was going to stay in my lane and compete with only myself because *I* am my only competition. Only I know where I've come from and where I plan to go and most of all, only God can judge me.

The problem these three C's cause in womanhood is in yearning for people's approval: Because there is nothing we won't do for it, especially degrading others for self-promotion. I'm not claiming all competition and comparison is negative but it should only be done when necessary. There's a lot of women out there that don't understand the difference between constructive competition, healthy comparisons, and uniqueness, and this results in just being plain mean to others or themselves. Competition and comparison could be beneficial if it was empowering or when it

~~

"Don't compare your beginning with someone else's middle."
-Jon Acuff

~~

is applied in a positive context, but if not, it is demolishing the most important things that make us happy and different (confidence, self-esteem, relationships, and friendships). So we compensate by attempting to level the playing field, do whatever to win, including getting other women "out of the way"...by looking better, cooking better, and being prettier than other women. Compare, compete, and defeat. Mission accomplished.

We see these three C's everywhere. The problem is, it's in places it definitely shouldn't be: like looks, personality, living for show, and dating. Just live within your means, look your best, and date by your standards and at your timing. These are the worst areas I see women yearning for attention and approval. So we have to do a better job at nipping it in the bud when we find ourselves doing these things, that's what makes a huge difference in our happiness. Stop when you find yourself doing it and correct it.

You don't want to be remembered as the one-upper or the complement-fisher, do you? A one-upper is a person that makes it a point to prove that they have done everything you have,

~~

"Don't measure your progress with someone else's ruler."
-Angelina Barlow

~~

only better and a million times more. For instance, if I say I wrote a book. The one-upper would say, Oh okay, I wrote six books last year and had a baby. There were no congratulations. No interest in what I wrote whatsoever. Notice this comment found a way to degrade my accomplishment by implying they did it six times and had a baby by the time I got one book out. What a jerk. The compliment-fisher is a person who goes out of their way for compliments and approval from others. They put on a little more makeup, buy the most expensive perfume in the department store, and they bring up their belongings or what they're doing to get a compliment or a bit of worship out of you. These types of people are obsessed with the public's opinion of them and obsessed with being in the spotlight all the time. It is something that can destroy your character, make you less fun to be around, and ruin your relationships.

~~

"Admire someone else's beauty without questioning your own."
-Chelsea Crockett

~~

In an age where social media is the key component of the three C's, we've made a new way to make each other look and feel terrible. Posting about every little thing that makes our lives perfect, posting half-naked pictures for likes, and leaving mean comments on other's statuses. It's like we forget the most obvious thing: people only post what they want you to see. It's all about that fake persona of perfection we talked about earlier, except now we are comparing and competing online. Stop letting other women's online lifestyles make you feel bad about your real life. Don't feed into it, because you don't know the full story and you have your own life to live anyway! And if the person really is that beautiful and happy just be glad for them and move on. We can all be great, there is nothing wrong with everyone being at their best at the same time. You need to focus on your life. You don't have to have one just like your friend has. It's possible that your story is just different. Be you. There is nothing wrong with being you because there's beauty in your life and who you are too! This is why we camouflage; we are afraid of ourselves

> *"2 Corinthians 10:12: Not that we dare to classify or compare ourselves with some of those who are commending themselves. But when they measure themselves by one another and compare themselves with one another, they are without understanding."*

if we are different and we are uninterested in what everyone else is doing, that's when you see that camouflaging. Are you picking up what I'm puttin' down?

You would feel a lot better if you'd stop masquerading your life for likes and follows on social media or for people's approval in general. In fact, just throw all that out the window, find what makes you happy and what you want to do and continue to do things in your life the way you have always done them. Don't compare, compete, or camouflage, and ruin yourself or your blessings in the process. And if you need to take a step back from social media and people as a whole because you feel yourself doing these things and letting it control you…do it! Social media is the enemy when it comes to these three C's but people fail to realize it could be the company we keep around us too.

Whew—I feel women love to compete with relationships on all platforms. You knew this relationship talk was coming in this chapter, sis. The reason being, relationships are one of the main places women are yearning for attention and approval, doing anything to win. When I was in college I had a friend that at one particular time I considered myself close

~~

"1 Thessalonians 5:16-18: Rejoice always, pray without ceasing, give thanks in all circumstances; for this is the will of God in Christ Jesus for you."

~~

to. She started "fooling around" with someone else on our track team and when she did that she constantly compared her not-really-a-relationship to my relationship all the time. I mean we could hardly even go on a double date because there'd be some type of crazy argument or comparison between the two couples at the table and it'd ruin the whole night. I think this friend was a little bit obsessed with these three C's and it didn't allow her relationship to be built on their foundation or their terms.

It was always like a contest or a race, trying to hurry up and catch up to where we were and do things the way we were doing things or better. However, what works for one relationship may not work for another. Long story short, I cut the toxic friendship. I figured I just didn't need that type of company around me.

Today, in womanhood if someone is still single at a certain age it is seen as a problem or that something must be wrong with them, but that is so untrue. Don't go chasing the approval of others by settling or camouflaging in the people you choose to be with and don't think there is a time frame where you should have it figured out just because that's what other women have.

You think just because your friend who has been with someone for one year gets married that you should too because you have been together for the same amount of time or longer? No, your life, your rules—being in love is not a contest and everyone loves at their own pace. To those of you saying you have tried relationships with different guys and are wondering what's wrong with you because your friend is already married:

Baby, there's nothing wrong with you other than the fact that you keep counting other people's blessings as what you should have.

~~

"Don't let your ice cream melt while counting someone else's sprinkles. - Akilah Hughes"

~~

I find sometimes that when a woman wants to be in a relationship so bad or wants attention, they start degrading themselves or others—especially on social media as we talked about just a minute ago. The amount of clothes being worn starts to become less and the posts start to become more frequent. Next thing I know I am seeing women in panties and bras laying in their bed every time I open Instagram competing for likes. Ladies, you don't have to disrespect yourselves to get approval or attention. You don't have to lower your standards at all.

Remember that the attention you are attracting going out every night and dressing sleazy is not husband material. Setting *thirst-traps* are only going to bring the *thirstiest* guys right to you. You don't want a guy trying to just quench his thirst because you are not a drink - you're a whole meal, okay? And do you think the future love of your life wants to see you posting half-naked for the world to see? Do you think it's fair for you to kill your self-worth just to be chosen as a prize? Don't camouflage and do what the others are doing, if you find yourself doing something to draw the wrong kind of attention, you probably shouldn't do it.

Now that we have talked about relationships, let's talk about another heart-wrenching thing women do with the three C's …personalities. "I wish I was outgoing like her. I wish I had a lot of friends like her. I wish I was attractive to guys like her…" Some women compare personalities and even try to act like someone they are not when around one another—for fame, for likes, for approval. The reasons could be a variety of things, maybe they want to impress one another, maybe they want to be popular and don't care about the bullying reputation they hold, or they want to impress men. That last one tends to be the case in most scenarios.

Have you seen the movie *Mean Girls*? If you have, you know what I'm talking about. There's a variety of scenes I could mention from the movie but I'll stick to the concept. It's in a high school where a bunch of catty girls want to be popular and pick on other girls to do it. It involves a whole girl posse who will do anything to be the trend. They even end up changing the nicest girl in school to be in their posse. You know what they say, "Birds of a feather flock together."I never even liked to have an entire girl posse follow me around and degrade other women to make ourselves feel like champs. I am a popular loner. You know, someone everyone knows but a person who doesn't hang out with a lot of

~ ~

"If you find yourself doing something to draw the wrong kind of attention, you probably shouldn't do it."

~ ~

people. Anyway, it's not something only younger women do, older women are guilty too. When my husband and I first moved to a new town, I had to start all over again like you always do when you move. I had to find everything again, from grocery stores, to church, to associates, to favorite places to hang out—you name it, it had to be re-established. The gym was no different. What we experienced there backs up my point about becoming bullies and acting like a hotshot.

The problem was that these women were simply too grown to be acting the way they were; they were between the ages of 60 and 80 years old! Remember I told you wisdom is not an automatic thing with age or living life. Anyway, I found a zumba class at this gym. When I went to zumba class for the first time, I had a great time and came home feeling kind of complete, as if I had found a new place to enjoy myself. So the next class I convinced my husband to join me. It was not easy to convince this 6'3" introverted black man to come to a zumba class. However, he loves me so much he went anyway. As we were minding our business and laughing about how ecstatic I was, these two ladies (who I will be calling grinches because they were grumpy and mean) approached us. One looked easily seventy-six years old, the other about sixty-five years old. The conversation went something like this:

Grinch #1: "Hi. Nice to see you again, but you guys are standing in our spots..."

Grinch #2 (adding her fuel to the fire): "Yeah, I normally stand in the front. Right here."

Then she pivoted her way in front of me.

My husband looked at me in disbelief, saying, "Did they just say that?" with his eyes.

Me: "Good evening to you too. I didn't see anybody's name anywhere."

Grinch #1: "Well we've all been coming to this class for years and everybody knows those are our spots. You are new so now you know. There are spots in the back."

Before I could say another word, the ladies stood in front of my husband. He looked at me and for a slight second, I paused and thought about cussing out these elders. My husband, not being dedicated to the fight because he wasn't that excited about zumba anyway, immediately gave in to these mean ladies and went to the back of the class. I on the other hand, as stubborn as I am, stood there glaring. That's when I looked them both dead in the face and said, "We pay to be here like everyone else! It's a first-come-first-served basis and we came here early to get spots with each other."

They ignored me and even started talking about us as if we weren't standing within earshot of their conversation. I yelled out, "You know we can hear you? If you have something to say, I'm standing right here. That's not very nice," with a look of disapproval.

My husband's eyes were opened wide with surprise. He probably thought I was about to throw down with these elders. But honestly, what would that look like? A young black woman, in decent shape, getting aggressive with two white senior citizens? It would've been all over the news. I just decided to leave. They killed our vibe. Let's see if I can ever convince him to go again.

The point I'm making with this scenario is that no matter how old women get, they bully other women with their so-called friends. They camouflage even if it's not who they are. However, real friends wouldn't expect you to behave this way, they'd actually tell you to stop. Friends are supposed to bring out the best in you, not the worst. I believe women should do that as a whole. I mean, why act like something you're not? These two were hyping each other up, pretending to be people they weren't. I told you I enjoyed that first class because the two of them weren't there together that night. It was just one of them and she was nice to me. There wasn't an issue with spots at all until her friends showed up and made it a big deal. Ladies just be you, don't *front*, don't switch up no matter who's around. Especially by being mean and putting down others. This makes me feel like we are a bunch of female peacocks. Flashing our feathers trying to impress each other.

So, you see this mentality is a problem, but we need to start finding a solution. This is a time to do a self-check.

We can avoid the three C's by sticking to these rules. Feel free to add your own if you feel I missed one:

a. **Counting your blessings (because everyone has their own) and being grateful** Remember that you can't claim other people's blessings and have no idea what they went through to get what they have! Learn to be grateful, thank God for what you have! Praise him for how far you have come and all the little things you're blessed with. Thank him for waking you up this morning, someone else is no longer breathing. See, there is positivity and self-assurance in measuring optimistically.

b. **Praying often, especially when you feel yourself becoming jealous of others** We all do it at times. The first step to progress is admission and then finding a technique that helps. Pray to God and ask Him to improve this harmful trait and to keep you grateful even when you want something someone else has.

c. **Stopping negative thoughts in their tracks and replacing them with good ones before they consume us** THIS ONE IS HUGE. It's so important to find the light in all situations especially when you think negatively about yourself, your life, or what you have. Remember that you have power in your thoughts. Control them by following up with a nice thought right after.

d. **Practicing confidence and positivity with soliloquizing** Talk to yourself! Tell yourself you've done a good job every once in a while and learn to hold your head up high because you're a queen. God said you were fearfully and wonderfully made so treat yourself like it!

e. **Thinking about how far we've come or what we have learned and how far we will go** Measure or compare where you came from to where you are today and compete with yourself to always improve. Those are healthy ways to use the three c's if you're going to do it at all.

f. **Not caring about other people's opinions and approvals** God created you and your unique story, life, and personality. His approval should be the only one that matters. He should always come before a person. God says we shouldn't want others' approval unless it's his. You know, only God can judge you. We've got to stop the circus act, the zoo, the high school replay, and empower ourselves by empowering one another.

g. **Meeting your expectations** If you are motivated by comparing yourself to others then you are living a lie. You are better off setting goals according to your own potential and desires. Live life for you!

h. **Being happy for others because you would expect the same** When someone shares their accomplishment or good news, congratulate them. It doesn't mean you aren't valuable because you didn't do the same. If you're trying to prove yourself in everything, you need to confront yourself and find out what's really going on.

i. **Picking up others when they are having a hard time** Everyone needs a shoulder to lean on sometimes. You have to remember we all have feelings and that we all mess up. So don't belittle someone when they make a mistake. Don't act like you're better than them, instead, tell them you've been there too. Here's a story about this rule: In third grade, I had a little friend who I won't be naming out of respect and privacy. She was small, quiet, and that made it easier for others to pick on her. So everyone in class gave her a hard time but she was my best friend. One day, my friend asked our teacher to go to the restroom. We're in third grade at the time, so you had to take the bathroom pass and raise your hand to ask for permission. So everyone knew that she needed to go, not making the next scene any easier.

She went to the restroom and when she came back found everyone in the class standing up, pointing, and laughing at her as she walked by to get to her desk. It seemed as if my friend had misused the toilet paper in the restroom. She had a trail of it following her from underneath her skirt. She was unaware and distraught. She didn't get why everyone was pointing and laughing at her. All the girls in the class stood up, pointing while calling her "sewer-skirt". She looked behind her to see a trail of toilet paper coming from between her legs. She was humiliated. She turned bright red and was so embarrassed she began to cry. She plopped down in her seat with a defeated look on her face. She put her head down. She didn't even try to fix herself. The teacher had to get the class to refocus. Soon enough, I asked to go to the restroom. I went into the stall, grabbed all the toilet paper I could, made the longest trail that I could underneath my skirt, and walked back into the class with a smirk on my face. Everyone stood up watching and looking to see that I had a trail underneath my skirt too. This time they laughed at me. I sat down right next to her and kept my toilet paper under my skirt until she decided to fix hers. Then and only then, would I have fixed mine.

Although my friend was now laughing uncontrollably and relieved, I got sent up to the office with a referral. When my mom found out she couldn't do anything but laugh. That night I told my mom, "Sometimes we all have toilet paper under our skirts too and don't know. I just wanted her to feel better." Life is hard and we don't need other women to make it harder. We should be in this together! I would put toilet paper under my skirt for you too, don't worry!

j. **Leading by example** The point is if we are displaying this type of behavior, others start to inherit it too. How do we expect to be treated like queens if we don't even do that for each other? The world would not be complete without women and we are the leaders of society. So, let's show each other that there is more to life, more to womanhood, besides competing, camouflaging, and comparing!

The harsh truth is that somebody will always have it better than you and someone will always have it worse. Why do you care? Why measure the value of your life and happiness by a system where the odds aren't for you or against you? That's just buffoonery. Think about a time where you've found yourself doing what we've talked about in this chapter.

Have you been a victim of the three C's? When have you compared yourself to another woman? How can you make sure you're not competing?

_____

_____

_____

_____

_____

_____

_____

_____

_____

_____

_____

_____

_____

_____

_____

_____

_____

_____

_____

CHAPTER 3

A King To A Queen

Remember how we used to play "house" when we were small? We had a mommy, a daddy, and the kids. Whether it be in a kid-sized playhouse in the back yard or with barbies bought for Christmas, we played this "house" game. Well, that same mentality has followed us into our adult lives, a wifey role, and a hubby role. But this time it's not meant to be all fun and games as stakes are higher and lives are invested. Exactly what led me to this chapter is women investing too much into the man who isn't worth it. It seems my fellow women don't know when they have been too good to the wrong man. Women are really out here doing things a wife would do for her husband, or playing "wifey" when the dude she is with simply doesn't deserve any of it! I'm seeing women

"When you learn how much you're worth, you'll stop giving people discounts."
Anonymous

over-sacrificing, giving their all, and lowering their standards for their current relationship. The problem is we're doing this for people who have no intention of marrying us or don't even deserve it. I have an example and it's quite hilarious.

I was born and raised in Arizona where an authentic Mexican restaurant called Filiberto's is located. I loved this restaurant so much that I would make it a routine to get tacos and burritos whenever I could. One day, the boyfriend I had (for three years) at the time and I decided to go there for their Taco Tuesday when their amazing tacos were roughly 39 cents. I ordered my typical four and he ordered his. While he was ordering and driving towards the first window, I started looking for my wallet. I was rummaging and rushing to find it, but didn't by the time we got closer to the window. I mentioned this to my boyfriend and the conversation went something like this:

Me: "I can't find my wallet. I think I left my wallet at home."

Him: "Why'd you leave without it? I guess you're not getting your tacos then."

I thought he was kidding until he looked away. I am already kind of shocked by the tone of his voice and the rudeness in his reply at this point. So I copped an attitude.

Me: "Excuse you, and you were rushing me. Can you just get the tacos for me? We are already here."

Him: "I don't feel like spending all that money to get you all those tacos. I'll just tell her you don't want them."

He pulled up to the window to pay for his food. The employee asks for about five dollars total for both of our tacos. I paused and looked at him...knowing five dollars is a small thing to ask for a three-year relationship and waiting to see what he would say.

Him: "How much were the three I ordered? She doesn't have the money for the other ones."

I am thinking *W-T-H. Is he serious? He's joking.*

Me: "So you really can't buy me four 39-cent tacos? How many times have I covered you for something? I sacrificed so much for you. You canceled my order and now you are just going to eat in front of me?"

He said thanks to the employee...he ignored everything I said.

A HUGE pet peeve of mine is to be ignored when I am talking to someone. The hot Arizona sun had nothing on the steam coming out of my ears at that point. I was hellish, truly angry.

I think he was behaving like a total creep, a chump. How many times has a man talked to you this way over something like this? This is a time to reflect, pause, and think about the real problem behind the argument. I saw it differently than he did. Yes, it was over tacos, but the true issue was that we were simply three years too far in the relationship to be arguing about something so little. I was flabbergasted.

For me, it was the fact that I had to ask, basically pull his teeth, to get him to do something he should be doing (he still didn't by the way)—having my back. What if it wasn't a taco? What if it was an emergency? Why was it an issue when I had done that same favor for him so many times before? You know, being boyfriend and girlfriend is the stage that shows you who you're dealing with. It allows you to see if you'd want to continue being with that person and maybe marry them. We were nowhere near that. I just felt humiliated and stupid for giving so much time to someone who couldn't even buy me 39-cent tacos three years later. I was over him at that point... that was all the sign I needed; after seeing so many red flags, that was the most ridiculous one.

No, I wasn't a shallow girl for breaking up with him for tacos. We had argued countless times about the relationship not progressing and me not getting the respect I deserved. There was even a time I walked away from him when I was upset and he shouted and whistled at me to come here. He demanded that I listen to him, like a dog. The relationship didn't meet the milestones and respect standards it needed to. It taught me what I wouldn't accept anymore.

So ladies, if you have ever been with someone like this you know how I was feeling. But some of you think this is okay or are too afraid to get out. It is not. It blows my mind to see how many women deal with men who don't try to be the best they can be for their women, they don't have your back and they take but never give. But you lie down with them and give them your taco. Sometimes conceive a whole child or marry him thinking that will make him better! Why do women think marrying a boy that is nowhere near being a man, or having his baby will mature him? You overcompensating for his lack of partnership will not make him better. *You can lead a horse to water but you can't force him to drink.* Girl, *if you don't drop him like a hot potato! I* would do it for you! So why don't you do it for yourself?

Women have to be smarter about when to bend over backward for their relationships. There are definitely points when you should do it and on the other hand big warning signs of when you shouldn't. For instance, dating is the time to find out if the relationship is going to work, but some signs cannot be ignored. At this time, you'll start thinking about settling down, moving in together, getting married, having kids, putting him on the lease or your insurance, cooking him

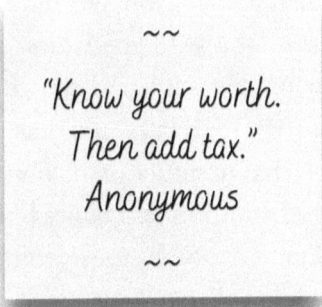

~~

"Know your worth. Then add tax."

Anonymous

~~

more dinners, delegating bills, you know all that adulting stuff. As a woman yearning to be in a healthy long-lasting relationship, it is significant, vital even, that we know when to play "wife" and how to do it in a healthy way for the RIGHT man. But BEFORE, not AFTER you do those things, make sure your man complies with your standards. Do not lower them to accommodate him. He shouldn't talk to you like a dog and not buy your tacos.

Warning signs are things like: cheating, lack of commitment, lack of responsibility, lack of manhood, lack of ambition, lack of respect, lack of compassion, etc. For example, if you're with a man who doesn't take care of his kids, doesn't have a stable job, acts like he is single, doesn't help around the house with bills or chores, doesn't plan on marrying you and doesn't even want to have the conversation, or just treats you like a booty call... don't ignore those signs and keep yourself in that relationship. He is not fit to be a husband or your king, so don't give him that luxury.

I have an intense story to share with you. I hope it makes the message clear. My old friend from high school asked me to share this with you ladies. To protect her privacy I am going to name her Sally and the guy Sam. Sally and Sam started with all the fairytales and kisses in their relationship. Sally soon started to notice Sam's obnoxious and flirty nature and that he had commitment issues but Sally hoped that she could change him—a mistake most women make. So she stayed and invested while Sam continued to show her all the red flags. Flirting with her friends, sisters, and classmates while in the relationship. They moved in together anyway. He didn't contribute to bills, she had a stable job so she paid for everything, cleaned up everything, cooked all the time, went to school, did all the managing a person could do and more. She eventually became pregnant. While she was practically acting like his wife (Even more than a wife because a wife and husband split or delegate household bills and duties...that wasn't even the case here as she was doing all the above.) She even found out Sam had an affair with her sister! Sam missed his baby's birth and didn't come to see her when she was hospitalized with the child. He just went about his life like he wasn't in a full-blown relationship. He wasn't ready for commitment and just didn't care to be. If Sally would have detached herself from him earlier she wouldn't have done all she did for this boy, including have his child. Now she knows her worth and knows what she won't tolerate but that didn't come without a lot of stress and regret.

Ladies, when you see the warnings continuously, you have to get out. A man will show you that he is not invested in you in several ways. While that Sally and Sam story may be a bit extreme for some of you, realize there are ladies out there really making this mistake or worse. I hope it's not you. If it is, you better act like you know your worth. You better stop taking his crap when you deserve gold. You decide what you tolerate and what kind of men you are in a relationship with. There is no excuse at all for you to degrade yourself by accepting anything less.

> ~~
> "You accepted less because you thought a little was better than nothing. Know your worth."
> Anonymous
> ~~

If he is acting like a little boy, then don't do it. You're not there to raise your man or train him to be what you want him to be. He should already be that way. Of course, he will learn things from you, but having to teach him right from wrong like a child is a nuisance. When and only when he respects you, contributes with you, is loyal to you, improves you, supports you, and prays with you shall you ever play "wife" for your man.

Listen, I am not saying you have to be married, be his baby's momma, or even have to have a child. The only requirement is that when he does things to enrich your life, then you let him in, then you show him you could be wifey. It will take months, maybe years before you start taking those steps.

Although the main goal is to be in a successful marriage for most women I understand that people may do things their way. I am not perfect as I was not married when I started doing more wifely things for my husband. We moved in together before marriage and we did things a married couple would do but very carefully in case it didn't work out. My husband and I did these things as a practice test before we got married. My biggest fear was to walk down the aisle with a man I hadn't gotten to know, only to find out he wouldn't contribute to the bills, wouldn't do things around the house, would take advantage of me, or have other issues. He obviously passed the test. He showed me no major red flags, promised me a future, always did his part or held up his end of the deal and said he planned for us to get married. Most of all, he respected me. He talked the talk, but he walked the walk too, by his actions.

~~

"Just say NO to complicated, dead-end, unhealthy, and toxic relationships."
Stephanie Lahart"

~~

If he wouldn't have promised me a future, contributed at home, had commitment issues, didn't treat me as a king should, or didn't return the favor of what I did for him, I would've been gone. My time is of the essence and I refuse to settle with someone who is not going to meet my standards. God said because I am a woman I am wonderfully made and some men can't handle all this wonderfulness. Unfortunately, I'm not seeing this same mentality in my sisters…this means you.

~~

""You're never asking for too much. You're just asking the wrong person."
-Kylie Francis"

~~

Don't be afraid to move on if he isn't what you need. You'll learn that your king is waiting out there if you let go of this peasant holding you back.

Why do you spend so much time with a man who doesn't plan on marrying you or doesn't deserve you anyway? Most of us dream of getting married and it is a goal of ours to be in a successful marriage. It just seems like that has changed nowadays as women are throwing that out of the window because some men don't want it. They start lowering those standards to be desirable to all men on the market. Don't change your goals of being a lifelong partner all because the guy you're with doesn't want that or seems to never be ready for that conversation. You deserve to ask him and deserve to know what his plans are for your life together or relationship. A real man, a king, can give you an answer or at least tell you he plans on being married one day if that is what he truly wants. All that playing around and avoiding commitment is for peasants. I know that was savage but you feel me?

Here are some sound examples of when I think you should "play" wifey:

1. He prays with you. (Personally, This is my number one. There is something so magical about praying together, about laying out all your worries as a couple and being patient enough to see them get relieved. I think it's best to be with a person who is spiritually connected.)

2. He has plans for the future! (BABYYYY! This is a biggy. If he knows what he is aiming for then he can lead the way for you as a man is supposed to do. He can be grounded enough to lift you to your goals. He knows what he wants in his future, so he will know what to want for his future family.)

3. He does not hit you, disrespect, or scare you. (He is not God and should not put fear in your bones. Honey, if he is yelling at you and putting his hands on you, you need to go.)

4. He encourages you or makes you better. (If he makes you worse or causes you to develop bad habits, kick him to the curb. He should better you 1,000%.)

5. He admits when he is wrong. (If he thinks he is always right and you are always wrong, get out. He won't take accountability or responsibility for his actions. That's a miserable situation to be in. It is emotional torture! Don't be emotionally abused and play wife for a man who doesn't know how to be husband material. You can play your role when he does.)

6. He does his part in the relationship. (All relationships are partnerships and need healthy slack and give-and-take. So if you find yourself giving to someone all the time who gives nothing in return, get out. If you find him slacking and you always pick up his slack, get out.)

7. He doesn't tell you you're "tripping" or you're "crazy" when you tell him how you feel. (That's a no-no. A huge pet peeve of mine is to be told I am tripping! Regardless of my personal feelings about it, it is actually wrong. You can't tell someone how to feel. You may not agree with the other person, but you can't tell them they don't have the right; we're human. It is saying that how *you* feel is worthless, invalidating what you have to say. It'll make you feel insignificant. He should listen to you even if he doesn't agree.)

8. He lets you be in charge too. (Don't let him call the shots all the time, you can call the shots too. When you step forward, he should step back, and when you step back, he should step forward.)

9. He quickly texts you back or picks up the phone when you call. AND he starts conversations too by calling you or texting you. (Communication is key. If the man is taking his sweet time to respond to you, he probably isn't that interested or maybe too busy to be in a fully-committed relationship.)

10. He doesn't threaten to break up with you every chance he gets. (That is a huge sign that he is unhappy and may even be into someone else. You need to step back

before you get burned. You probably should leave him if he is saying he'll break up with you every time you get into a little argument.)

11. He takes you out. (He should be taking you to restaurants, movies, or whatever you guys like to do on dates. He needs to hang out with you, have fun, and be comfortable doing it too.)

12. He is proud of you. (He should be eventually taking you to meet his friends and family, not getting mad if you want to post a random selfie with him, and he should be happy calling you his woman.)

13. He tells you or shows you how he feels about you and not with descriptions that sound like he is talking to his homeboys. (What I mean by homeboy descriptions is something that sounds like this: "we chillin', I think you're cool." Let him know you won't be taking any of his crap if he can't even answer your question respectfully.)

14. He has a respectful family and respects his family. (If a man was raised by a jacked-up family, he's probably gonna be jacked-up. Pay attention to his family and how he treats his mom because that is how he'll treat you.)

15. He is not cheating on you and entertaining all the flirty girls in the world. (You should feel confident that your man only wants you. Some women won't respect it but he shouldn't betray your trust or even make you feel like he would the first chance he gets. Don't live a life where you are constantly walking on eggshells.)

Ladies be picky! You are wifey material. You are a Queen, remember? But why be all that for a loser? For a man who is a peasant and not a king. For a boy who is not "hubby" material? You better recognize your value!

When have you been too good to the wrong man? What have you tolerated even though you shouldn't have? How will you treat yourself more like a Queen?

CHAPTER 4

Get Out Your Feelings!

Girls. Feelings. They go hand-in-hand...and because, of the two sexes, we are more in tune with our emotions we are more likely to find ourselves lacking logic because of how we feel. We immediately respond when we should pause and think, *What should I do or what would I do if I was not so high on emotions?* You know, think about your principles. Sometimes we get lost in the motion of emotion, at least I do. That is not to say men don't have feelings and are complete saints, that's not true at all. Men have their issues with letting feelings in other ways lead them right into trouble. Do you feel me? However, this book isn't for them, it's for us Queens, remember? When I talk about being lost in our feelings, I'm not talking about just PMS mood swings, but actually making decisions and acting out solely because we let our emotions control our reasoning

> ~~
>
> *"For God gave us a spirit not of fear but of power and love and self-control."*
> 2 Timothy 1:7
>
> ~~

and that usually leads to overreacting and doing something we'll regret. We have to be more selective about what gets a response. A good man once told me, "Think twice, speak once." Not every little thing needs a response. We have to stop letting our crowns get crooked about things that don't even deserve a reaction. Queens, let's practice being unbothered and remember how royal we are.

I'm a lover of raw unedited poetry and its richness of feelings. This is because I am a ball of feelings: sensitive, irritable, hyper, sad, sometimes laughing and crying at the same time, I do whatever feels right. I am a hot mess and while I know that, it doesn't give me the right

> ~~
> *"You don't have to control your thoughts, you just have to stop letting them control you." - Dan Millman*
> ~~

to always behave that way. I'm just downright emotional. I sometimes don't even know why I am feeling the way I do at a particular time and don't have control over my feelings at all. However, I am slowly learning to not let my emotions have control over me. Assuming control over my emotions has been a battle I've been fighting my whole life. For a while, I thought something was wrong with me but I've come to find out, as I am living life and bonding with other women, a lot of women have this same issue—letting our feelings rule us!

Oftentimes, letting your feelings be your boss can leave you treading thin water, losing self-control, peace, and eventually doing something we'll later regret. There's a little song I'd like to sing to you as an example:

"I bust the windows out ya car

And no it didn't mend my broken heart

I'll probably always have these ugly scars

But right now I don't care about that part..."

I Bust The Windows Out Your Car, sang by the smooth and strong Jasmine Sullivan. It's one of my jams, but it leaves me thinking about the decisions women make when we're in our feelings. We need to learn to get out of our feelings sometimes!

A few stanzas later she says plain as day "But it didn't comfort my broken heart." Backing my point, of the futility of acting out of bare emotion. She found out that busting the windows out of her man's car in pure rage helped to channel that anger somewhere, but didn't help the situation after all. It left her feeling the same way if not worse and had him looking at her crazy. That's the problem, feelings should be governed by reason and truth. Obviously, in this case, like most, it was definitely not.

Oh, that's just one example. Trust me, I've got more! My friend and I talked just the other day about this. She told me a story

~~

"Proverbs 29:11: A fool gives full vent to his spirit, but a wise man quietly holds it back.

~~

47

about her emotions getting the best of her and I couldn't do anything but laugh and agree. She was at home with her man and cooking dinner when she decided to walk over to him, he was sitting at his computer. She stood behind him and rested on his shoulders. She noticed his phone lit up and a woman's name she had never seen before, was on the screen. The contents of the message led her to believe they were getting together or just had. Immediately, she got suspicious, irritated, and her emotions turned for the worst. Heated, she walked away back into the kitchen. Now cooking dinner, in silence, temper rising, with an attitude. She had already made up her mind that he was flirting or entertaining another woman. Again her feelings were not governed by reason or truth. At least, she didn't know that yet. What made the issue worse was that he had no idea that she was upset. That was until she lashed out and went on a rampage of questions backed by assumptions or conclusions she came up with on her own! After he could finally get a few words in, he asked her to calm down and proceeded to tell her the new name that popped up on his phone was a person he was introduced to as a long-lost relative at a family gathering. By now my friend was embarrassed and apologized for making a complete fool out of herself, jumping to conclusions, and saying things she regretted. We might be murmuring, *I don't do that* but the truth is others see things clearer from an outside perspective. When you were reading that it was probably a-hundred-percent obvious that she shouldn't have behaved that way but that's because you're on the outside. What if you approached every situation that way? What if you ask yourself, *I wonder how I'd look to the neighbors right now if I busted the windows out of my boyfriend's car?*

You also know what I've noticed? We always skip the benefit of the doubt when we are totally pissed or sad. Why do we skip the benefit of the doubt? Make fools of ourselves? Why is it that women don't need evidence or proof before we conclude? How is it that in these circumstances, we're not able to reel it back in? It's in our nature. We can't help but get caught up in emotions but that doesn't mean we should accept it and let our feelings have us all willy-nilly. There's another song by Jhene Aiko that makes me laugh because it is so true for most women. It's called *Hello Ego:* "Ima be real real real real honest I got some real real real real real problems. I just do what I feel I don't deal with no logic. I need to chill. I need to chill. I need to stop it. Need to stop it now."

Sometimes when we make decisions based on emotions we don't think about the future or the outcomes, we just want to feel better at that time. Another reason why we most likely act out of emotion is because of doubt or insecurity. Every woman has doubts or insecurities; as I said, no one is perfect. Sometimes these doubts or insecurities have legitimate reasons for why they exist, you could have

~~

"Some people use their own hurt as an excuse for hurting others."
— Rolland Merullo

~~

been hurt badly in the past, or grappled with something in the past that leaves you a little sensitive. If you are hurt, you will hurt others. You know what they say: hurt people, hurt people. While other times there's not a legit reason at all. We don't always have the right reaction or even the right answer, but God already knows we have this issue and that's why he offers so much sound advice in the Bible for not letting a stirred-up spirit, heart, or emotion get the best of you. I know we can't pick up the Bible

~~

"I don't want to be at the mercy of my emotions. I want to use them, to enjoy them, and to dominate them. — Oscar Wilde"

~~

at every single moment we are pissed but an effective mental check could be a simple reminder that anything extreme is a no-no

We need to be better at controlling the things that we can control, and that is us. You can't control the mishaps of life, you can't control the way you feel, but you can control the way you respond to the emotional pain. You can help if these things get the best of you. You need to go to the best therapist on the block and that is God. You can confide in friends, see an actual therapist, and all that, but until you activate God's word about conquering the battle of feelings, you won't see a change. Take it from me as I have a hard time with one particular feeling, sometimes for no reason: jealousy. I had my come-to-Jesus moment after I had taken things too far and overreacted with my man various times. Probably more than I could count.

I love my husband, he is easy to love and very attractive and I believe he is one of the best things that has ever happened to me. I know other people find my husband lovable and just as handsome as I find him and that can kind of be scary when driven by insecurity. So, I've acted out on this feeling of jealousy, the moment I see hearts, blushy faces, or anything that looks even remotely flirtatious, being sent to him from a female, I'm immediately annoyed. I've even gotten upset with him to the point where I have started an argument. I've got a lot of attitude and a feisty mouth when emotions get the best of me. Did I end up saying hurtful things, all over emojis? And all over things he didn't even do? Yes, and yes. It was SOMEONE ELSE who sent these to him. He never sent them back or even acknowledged them.

Sidenote: Kudos to my husband for not telling me to chill when I was ripping him a new one but then again he knows that can send me to a crazy place I may not return from for a while. However, he was very frustrated and annoyed with me for yelling and being mean to him

"Matthew 18:21-22: Then Peter came up and said to him, "Lord, how often will my brother sin against me, and I forgive him? As many as seven times?" Jesus said to him, "I do not say to you seven times, but seventy times seven.

about something so small. It's just at that moment it didn't feel small. It never does, right? He figured I should know he wouldn't do anything to jeopardize our relationship. The big whammy he hit me with is don't punish him for something he didn't do all because I jumped to a conclusion. There wasn't any tangible evidence that he was flirting, or even entertaining it, maybe the emoji-sender could be flirting but the big takeaway is that he wasn't!

After everything calmed down, I did some self-reflection. I'm stubborn so it takes me a while. I have to sit with myself and let it marinate. I asked myself if those emojis were that troubling and of course, I came

~~

"Be angry and do not sin; do not let the sun go down on your anger."
- Ephesians 4:26

~~

to the conclusion that no, they weren't that troubling. It wasn't that serious and I was just in my feelings about something my husband could care less about. I cried, said sorry, prayed, and took up the Bible. I realized that acting out when I have these negative emotions could be hard for my loved ones to deal with. As I said, this is just one little example, I have done this many more times. I am better now though. I'm not saying I've gotten better overnight, or even that I have control over my emotions. It's been an uphill war for me but the Bible scriptures and quotes you see in this chapter are very personal reminders for me and that's why I chose to share them with you. God has been my deliverer and savior in these ongoing battles. He has always reminded me to not be prideful and to have a heart of forgiveness and reconciliation (I'm not saying be a pushover, but respond in a smart manner, if the situation even calls for a response in the first place). So sometimes we've got to step back, leave the premises, think, pray, and then come back. Why do I bring up pride? Well, we are not God...sin is

~~

"James 1:19-20:
"Know this, my beloved
brothers: let every person be
quick to hear, slow to speak,
slow to anger; for the anger
of man does not produce the
righteousness of God."

~~

against God, not us. We have a pride issue because we feel we are entitled to react however we want. Push that pride to the side. If God has to deal with things that make him upset why would you think you don't have to? Does he respond all crazy every time you do something he doesn't like? No. He knows anybody is capable of sin and we have to remember anybody is capable of hurting us or messing up sometimes, the same way God acknowledges those tendencies.

"How can we get better?" is the obvious question. I've come up with steps for myself when I feel my emotions getting the best of me and I can say that ever since I've followed them, I haven't acted in a way I regret. I've found more self-control. I call them *chill-checks.*

<u>Chill-Checks</u>

1. Pray (If you want to yell, scream, talk, do that with God. Tell him how you're feeling and get those burdens off your chest. He is an amazing listener.)

2. Read specific anecdotes and apply them to everyday life. There are some in this chapter!

3. Memorize those anecdotes and activate them at the most difficult times until they become second nature.

4. Pause and practice self-control.

5. Don't take things personally (Is the offense a direct attack on you? If it is, think about how to respond BEFORE you do it.)

6. Don't jump to conclusions (Think about the benefit of the doubt. Come up with "maybes" but don't just make a snap decision that you know exactly what's going on...because you probably don't. They say there are three sides to a story: your side, their side, and the truth!)

7. Check the facts or evidence (Would it be obvious to you if someone else was in your shoes? You know, that outside perspective we talked about. Or is it just a sore spot for you? Is there proof that supports your reaction?)

8. Address your insecurities (Find out why you're insecure about the things you are and do things that make you feel more secure in yourself. Remind yourself that you're a Queen and that you must only react when necessary.)

9. Choose when to react, instead of always reacting.

10. Repeat (Keep using these tactics until it becomes second nature.)

So, there you have it. A deeper, more complicated part of womanhood. I believe in us though. We just have to take it day-by-day. It's okay if you feel some type of way but don't be ruled by those emotions. So just relax and get out of your feelings, girl.

When have you unnecessarily jumped to conclusions? How have emotions gotten the best of you? How will you get better?

_____

_____

_____

_____

_____

_____

_____

_____

_____

_____

_____

_____

_____

_____

_____

_____

_____

_____

CHAPTER 5

The Past and The Present Don't Mix

"*B*ag Lady...
You gone hurt yo' back

Draggin' all them bags like that

I guess nobody ever told you

All you must hold onto - is you, is you, is youuu!"

These are lyrics from one of my favorite songs by the soulful Erykah Badu. This song hits exactly what I'm going to talk about in this chapter, which is how women keep carrying around emotional baggage or grudges from the past into their present romantic relationships. Emotional baggage or grudges are unresolved, unsettled, or unforgiven issues. These issues that induce baggage or grudges come from any

~~

"You can't start the next chapter of your life if you keep re-reading the last one.
- Anonymous

~~

negative experiences ranging from childhood to adulthood. To set the record straight, carrying baggage will most likely happen at some point in your life, but letting it control your relationships is not okay. I get it, negative experiences suck but you can't let them determine you or your life. We've got to let it go and move on. Carrying around all those bags will eventually get too heavy and weigh us down.

The most common type of baggage or grudges derive from abuse. It could be mental, emotional, or physical abuse. We will tap more into this in a later chapter, but for now, let's just keep it at a topical level. If you ever experienced or witnessed any type of abuse in your life, odds are you have carried your fears, pain, and emotional turmoil into your romantic relationships. Abuse could come from either of the sexes, but women take it harder when it comes from a male, as we believe that they are supposed to be protecting us. Most women search for leadership and protection in their relationships. So, it's sad to think we have grown used to being hurt and disappointed. Childhood trauma is another big part of baggage or grudges. If you experienced abuse in your childhood and never confronted it, you could be taking your anger and fear out on any guy you've ever been serious with. There are many negatives. Kids can suffer from social and emotional neglect. However, childhood trauma doesn't automatically connect with abuse, it could be neglect, mental illness, or abandonment. Neglect and abandonment were my issues for a long time as one parent decided to throw me to the wolves. It happened to be my father, who was supposed to protect. My childhood trauma involved me growing up without a strong father figure or a father at all. Just searching on Google you could see that about 25% of kids grow up in a single-parent household. It is typically with their mothers. I grew up with a single mother who had it hard raising my brother and me. We stopped getting support from our father, and my mom worked up to three jobs at one point to keep food on the table. I stayed home with my brother, who is seven years younger than me, playing mommy at a young age. I warmed up dinner my mom made us before she jetted off to work, got us showered, changed diapers if needed, did our homework, and got us ready for school the next day. My granddaddy was there most times but he normally would be knocked out on the couch. Gotta love that man. There were nights we had no electricity or hot water. We scraped up change to pay for necessities at times because we didn't have money like the other families. We practically lived at the dollar store. This all caused me to step up as a young girl, which would be overwhelming for any child. It's why I grew up to be distrusting of any males, insecure, and too independent. You can imagine how that baggage caused issues in any serious relationship. The lack of a father figure made it harder for me to trust others and be emotionally available, it made me expect all men to abandon me at some point in their lives, too independent, scared of commitment myself, and too ready to cut someone off within a blink of an eye. Being such an independent person can make you incapable of working as a team with your significant other. It can be hard to deal with and even make you self-centered. Well, that was my world. I didn't constantly have a good man or role-model as a partner around me growing up, as many women do. They learn what a good partner is by seeing it in their parents' relationships. I didn't know what a good man was and even when approached with one, I would self-sabotage because of my emotional warfare.

This reminds me of a movie I love to watch. It stars Idris Elba and is written by Tyler Perry. Ever heard of *Daddy's Girls*? A young black father separates from the mother and meets a

~~

"Let go of the past, but keep the lessons it taught you.
-Anonymous

~~

headstrong attorney, who happens to be played by Gabrielle Union, falls in love with her and she ends up saving his three little girls from their mother and her drug-dealing boyfriend's household of physical and emotional abuse. The father gains full custody and takes care of his babies. I used to wish my father would try to see me and maybe even spend weekend visits with me. Then I realized the way I looked at it made a huge difference. I pretended my mom was Idris Elba in a way, because that woman…she would save me from anything. Once, after I met my husband, I had a personal conflict that I was struggling with and he helped me through it. I have respect for him because of how much he has taught me, how patient he has been, and his maturity has made me better. He helped heal me and no matter what happens between us, I admire him for that.

Baggage or grudges could also contribute to physical health complications. The University of Minnesota conducted a study on this topic. Here's a quote from that study which struck me most: "Poorly-managed negative emotions are not good for your health. Negative attitudes and feelings of helplessness and hopelessness can create chronic stress,

~~

"Sometimes people with the worst pasts end up creating the best futures.
-Anonymous

~~

which upsets the body's hormone balance, depletes the brain chemicals required for happiness, and damages the immune system."

Notice in my example it wasn't a romantic relationship that had me carrying around baggage or grudges, it was a male figure, or the lack thereof. I find my situation to be less common, as women mainly carry around fears and pain from failed or chaotic romantic experiences. However, don't count me out of that one either as the first relationship I was in, I got cheated on. That was hard too because I learned to put aside my fears and emotional turmoil from being neglected by my father to give dating a try. My first breakup was terrible. I thought I was going to die and to be honest that really doesn't go away when you're older, you just learn how to adapt. But at this time I was sorely convinced that I'd stay with this young man forever. He was my first "love". I was fantasizing over some Romeo and Juliet stuff. I was about 17 years old and we held hands all the time. We went on walks all the time. He even enjoyed the same sports that I enjoyed. So we had a good time. We had a lot in common. He liked me so much until one day he decided he didn't anymore and he just abandoned me without an explanation, just like my father!

He went MIA on me out of nowhere. He wouldn't text me or call me back. He wasn't home when I went to see him. He didn't sit with me at lunch at school…it was so odd. I felt even worse because everyone that knew us saw him around except me. I knew he was avoiding me but just couldn't figure out why. He texted me and said he was bored with me. When I replied and tried to solve the issue, he never replied and went missing again. He ended up having sex with a girl that was on one of our sports teams the next day. Do the math, while we were together he had sex with another female! I was devastated when he told me over text that he had gotten with her. Now my mom was on some straight G stuff as usual when I told her about it. She said "Uh-uh." Anything that he left at our house from coming over, she packed up in a brown grocery store bag. The next day she showed up to our practice where he was googly-eyeing the girl right in front of me. This is how it all went down:

All I saw was this little blob of a human strutting towards the field, looking pissed and walking with a mission, fast as a bullet, as determined as a bull heading straight towards us. I didn't get it at first but as I squinted to make out who this person was walking angrily towards the field it occurred to me that it was my mom! Oh *lord*.

She stormed right over to him and his friends. She threw the plastic bag of his clothes at him and said, "My daughter said get the hell out. You dirty." Everybody shouted "OOOHH! BURNNN!! DAMN BRO!" Then she turned around, winked at me, and walked right back in the direction she came. This time more satisfied in her strut. Straight savage.

Now when you're in high school and your mom does something like this it is epic. My mom straight up told this boy about himself in front of his friends. I loved her for that and I still love her for that. The news spread like wildfire on campus and the next day everyone was talking about it. He came and apologized for the way it all went down.

My mom is a no-nonsense type of person and that's where I get it from. Anyway, I was so hurt and embarrassed, I stayed in my room crying. I didn't want to go outside, I didn't want to hang out with my friends. Because at any given moment I was on the verge of tears. Let me give you a weird example: when I came out one day for my room to get breakfast I was greeted so nicely by others in the house because I hadn't come out of my room in days. I went to get something to eat and they started teasing me about nothing at all and even nudging me a little bit to get me to smile. I was so sorely hurt by my breakup I busted up into tears and ran back into my room. I didn't want to go to practice. I didn't want to go to school because he would be there. I was embarrassed that he would do that to me. My heart felt like it got ripped out of my chest. I had a negative perception about guys after my first boyfriend cheated on me, it kind of set the tone.

You will always have negative experiences that can become baggage or grudges if you allow them to. Some people allow these bad experiences to become baggage or grudges that they carry for years! That's exactly what I did with both of those experiences. I know my story isn't from a marriage or twelve-year relationship in my thirties but it still hurts me. While some of you may have had more dramatic experiences, I know you're still picking up what I'm putting down.

Baggage or grudges is obviously a problem. However, the negative occurrences that create them are not always 100% negative. It helps you to discover your boundaries, find out what you want, and establish expectations. As for those negative experiences taking a toll on your love life, there are things we can do to make it better:

1. Acknowledge that you have a grudge or emotional baggage. While you're there you might as well find out the problem or the lesson.

2. Forgive. Let me tell you this is the hardest one for me! It still takes longer than I would like to forgive someone who hurt me. But put it this way, a smart guy once told me that we are not God and for us to hold grudges or not forgive someone that is also human, as if we don't make mistakes, is foolish. Humans even turn their backs on God and he forgives them if they just acknowledge they messed up. So why can't we do the same? God tells us how terrible it is to not forgive.

3. Let it Go! This coincides with number 2. You can do it. If a person apologizes and acknowledges their mess-up, you can at least be cordial with them. You can also let

them earn your trust again. Don't keep "rubbing their nose" in their mistake or even rubbing the next guy's nose in it.

Take it from Erykah Badu, all you must hold onto is you! Pack light and go into your future or current relationship without that grudge or baggage.

What have you held a grudge about? How have past relationships shaped your current relationship? What are the pros and cons of a negative experience you've encountered? How have you ever self-sabotaged a relationship?

_____

_____

_____

_____

_____

_____

_____

_____

_____

_____

_____

_____

_____

_____

_____

_____

_____

_____

CHAPTER 6

If he wants you, he'll show it.

We already talked about women overcompensating for guys that don't give them half of what they deserve. But what really "grinds my gears" is when a woman does all this for a guy who won't even put a title on it. A guy she is just "talking" to. You know, entertaining as if they are in a relationship although they have no title. We are so desperate for good that we paint over a bad man with a figment of our imaginations of a good one. I see it happening all around me. It's been me. I am telling you if he wants you he'll meet your standards, he'll claim you, and he'll

~~

"Love yourself enough to set boundaries. Your time and energy are precious. You get to choose how to use it. You teach people how to treat you by deciding what you will and won't accept."
-Anna Taylor

~~

show it! If he doesn't show it and doesn't make you his, he doesn't want you. I mean what is his endgame? Think about it, if it isn't clear—it's clear. You need to leave him alone. Men move at their own pace for their own reasons. Nothing you can do can make him show that he wants you. Sorry girl, I am here to break the news to you because I am on your side.

Have you seen the movie Friends With Benefits, starring Justin Timberlake and Mila Kunis? It's centered around these two friends who start sleeping together with no expectations or strings attached. It starts out all fun and games until real feelings develop and "ruin" their arrangement. They eventually have to make a decision to 1) be friends knowing they want to be more 2) be in a relationship or 3) not be around each other at all because it became too awkward. But why did they put themselves in a predicament where they had to choose? Luckily, they end up with each other but in real life, the third option is usually what happens.

Like this movie, I've seen it happen to my friends or family and a variety of women I know. You'll find so many women out there have been in the same position. I see people hang out every day, pay bills together, run errands like going to the grocery store, sleeping over at each other's houses on a nightly basis, all the couple stuff you could think of, and still claim they're just friends with this pained look on the women's faces. Friends with benefits, "talking", being in a "situationship", or whatever you want to call it, still doesn't make it a relationship. It remains untitled, unsupported, unacknowledged and incognito. Baby, he sees you as incognito! This "we're just talking" attitude is nothing but a nervous, desperate-for-love-but-not-the-commitment rollercoaster. I was on it too, but I had to get off because all the bobbing, weaving, ducking, and diving was making me sick! I get sick just seeing other ladies putting themselves through it.

Those same ladies I mention in this position are left asking the same question—*What are we?* Where on the ladder am I? Honestly, how the hell do you walk a blurred line? The answer from the guy is always "we just talk or we're just friends." All this question does is irritate me when I hear it because honestly, why should you even have to ask? Go with your gut feeling, your 'feelings brain' and use common sense. He hasn't asked you to be his lady because you already give him all of the luxuries of having a lady without a relationship. That's like getting free gas and not having to pay for it. Would you walk into the store and tell them you've been getting free gas and would like to start paying for it? If a store associate hasn't come out and said you need to start paying you're going to keep pumpin'. Same in a situationship...we shouldn't have to ask because we should already know where we stand. Maybe the fact that you're asking *is* the answer. You're not in a relationship if you have to ask. Remember I told you I'm keeping it one-hundred.

> ~~
> *"Don't let the mixed signals fool you. Indecision is a decision."*
> *–Anonymous*
> ~~

I've been there too. Actually, I was there with my now-husband almost five years ago. It started with all fun and games but my feelings got attached quickly. He told me he didn't know about any of the relationship stuff yet

~~

"Don't let anyone that doesn't value you, determine you're worth."
-Anonymous

~~

when I asked him that famous question. I told him my heart and time were nothing to play with so he had two choices: 1) get with it or 2) get to steppin'. He chose to get with it and has been with it ever since. There were guys who didn't get with it and I stopped fooling around with them immediately. I didn't want to waste time and talk or date forever. It gets old. I was hurt at that time and confused. I shed tears and wasted a couple of years entertaining guys who just wanted booty calls and nothing more but after a couple guys dogged me, I told myself, *never again*. Shortly after, I met my husband, who wouldn't say anything about a relationship, and the feelings sprung back up and I said no I am not doing this again and said: "Get some balls and tell me what it is that we are doing. If you are a friend I will treat you like it. If you want to be my man, good for you. But you can't have your cake and eat it too." I would have pushed him to the side if he didn't claim me just like I did with the others.

Every time I've asked one of my girlfriends why they put themselves in such a painful situation, they all say the same thing. I said the same thing. They accept it because they want him or see the potential. They want any part of him they can get even if that leaves them with basically nothing but a broken heart. They still take it because they think that little bit is better than nothing. How do you still come up short when you give everything? How is everything not enough? I'll tell you why, because you could do everything and still mean nothing to a man who won't even give you a title!

I think another reason why women accept this situation is that they think they don't deserve answers. However, that is so untrue. As a person laying their feelings, time, money, and energy all on the line, you do deserve to know answers. Maybe he just doesn't have them, so be with someone who does.

The real problem with this situation is that you are holding him up to relationship standards even though you're not in a relationship. You aren't doing anything but setting both of you up for failure. You don't know what you are to him or where you guys are going. It's like driving down a road blindfolded: stupid and dangerous! For guys, it seems like a win-win. Guys these days want to be

~~

"there's nothing more confusing and painful to a woman than being told that she's amazing by a man who treats her like she's not good enough to commit to."
-r.h. Sin

~~

single but enjoy all of the luxuries of being in a relationship without the attachments and responsibilities. However, for us, it's a situation that gives no clarity. And having no clarity leads to chaos or us getting hurt. Ladies, we are trying to get to the top of the ladder of relationships, aren't we? We are trying to get to the last stage of a relationship: marriage and forever. We don't have time to waste. It normally ends horribly but for some reason, women agree to it anyway. And if they don't agree they find themselves in the middle of it not knowing what to do. Even if you don't actively agree to it and you just passively allow yourself to be in that situation, you kind of still agree to it because you stay. However, what I hate the most is when we women act like we want this too...because we really don't. We act like we just want to be friends and sex buddies to keep him around. We act like we don't want something serious like a committed relationship. And don't lie to me, or lie to yourself by saying you do! I don't want that for you!

Why do you want it for yourself? We know it's a problem but how do we fix it?

1. **Put yourself first.** Apply that time and energy you are spending with that drain of a human to your career, talent, and betterment.

2. **Start having higher expectations for your relationships.** If you settle for less that is what you will ALWAYS get. Men know who they can bull crap with. You might as well nip it in the bud.

3. **Don't you dare beg or chase him.** A man will move when he wants to. Your crying, nagging, arguing, and

overcompensating will not make him love you. It will not make him move. No more begging him to put a title on it because there is a man out there who will do that for you gladly without you even asking. Put it this way, Queens do not beg and do not chase, it is beneath us.

4. **Stop being naive.** You are a "whole" grown woman, don't be gullible. Check his actions and the facts and if it doesn't add up, don't believe his bull crap.

5. **Stop being strung along and hoping for the best.** Women are living off of the potential the relationship could have instead of focusing on what it is—a bunch of nothing! We just talked about getting out of your feelings; look at what's in front of you. Don't let the way you feel cloud your judgment.

6. **Be transparent always, especially to yourself.** Tell him what you want or expect and ask him the same thing. Tell him you don't want lies, but the truth.

7. **Don't make excuses for this grown man.** It is what it is. He isn't stupid, he knows what he is doing. He's gaming you and you are not meant to be played. No matter what he's been through, it doesn't give him a right to hurt you!

8. **Keep your options open!** Do not stop yourself from going on dates because you don't know what's going on with you and ol' boy. I hate to see women shut down nice guys all for a crappy one who doesn't know what to do with you. Take the opportunities to hang out with

friends, get your work promotion or relocation, and move on with your options.

9. **You have to know when to draw the lines or enforce boundaries.** Don't let him have his cake and eat it too.

10. **If he wants to be friends, treat him like a friend!**

11. Queen, adjust your crown, get back on your high horse and ride away back to your castle. A part of being royal is being savvy, knowing attackers and jokers when you're dealing with them. Keep your head, heels, and expectations high! If he wants you, he'll show it.

~~

"Don't let anyone that doesn't value you, determine you're worth."
-Anonymous

~~

Have you ever been or are you in one of these "situationships"? How did/
does it make you feel? How will you treat yourself more like a Queen?

_____

_____

_____

_____

_____

_____

_____

_____

_____

_____

_____

_____

_____

_____

_____

_____

_____

_____

CHAPTER 7

Partnerships vs. Relationships

"We never wanted a divorce at the same time, so we went the distance," wrote Kathleen Rowell in a diary entry back in 2017 about how her marriage has lasted as long as it has. To date, she has been married for about 47 years. It's interesting to me that she and her husband are still married; even though they may have wanted a divorce at one point in time, they STILL didn't do it. Divorces are so normal in this day and age and are easily obtained. And the resulting hike in divorce rates just keeps climbing. Regardless of what the world said or how this couple felt at one particular time, they stayed partners.

This is the same conversation I had with my sister-in-law one day as she gave me the rundown on being partners. She's been married for almost 30 years. That's the same

~~

"Forget a relationship Make it a Partnership And Build an Empire."
-Anonymous

~~

powerful message my husband's uncle and his wife of over 64 years gave my husband and me at our wedding! It's kind of funny that when I ask people who have been married for my whole age or more, they all kind of give me the same answer—that a relationship is nothing without a partnership; but that they are two different things! Anybody can be in a relationship but it takes structure and hard work to be in an ongoing partnership. Divorces are like pulling the trigger while partnerships are like glue holding it together. It's kind of like looking at it as a lease, you sign for another year if you really enjoyed the last one.

These talks have a deep meaning to me as I am in my late twenties and married, hoping and praying to make it to where these couples are one day. I can't help but feel since I've taken their advice and added to it for my marriage, that it's true. It's the mentality I had five years ago

~~

"Ecclesiastes 4:9: Two are better than one, because they have a good return for their labor: If either of them falls down, one can help the other up. But pity anyone who falls and has no one to help them up. Also, if two lie down together, they will keep warm. But how can one keep warm alone?"

~~

when I started dating my husband, I just hadn't put a name to it yet and it didn't seem as important until I heard these things from someone else's mouth.

I think the problem that makes it so hard to think about a partnership, is the societal acceptance of divorces, not getting married, and just break-ups in general. It's like the words marriage and partnership have been cheapened. This pressure has people either getting married for the wrong reasons, not getting married at all, or leaving for the wrong reasons. I've Googled divorce rates and noticed the slow rise and fluctuation but what really stood out to me is fewer people are getting married and a lot of the people that are getting married aren't staying married. Divorces are currently rated at 3.2 per 1,000 population and marriages have been at their lowest since 1867! I think it comes down to this: People are holding off marriage. It's only amplified in my generation…music, drugs, TV, movies, politics—all of it influences us to party harder, date more, make bad decisions while we are young, and fear commitment. However, when the music dies and the party's over, who's going to be there? What do you want to do, date forever? Then what? Why fear commitment? Because people fear abandonment, vulnerability, boredom, freedom, time, baggage, and have trust issues. You name it, I've heard it. People are scared of putting in all the time and effort and their spouse just walking away. And don't get me wrong, these are good reasons to be afraid but most of them have simple solutions, are out of your control, or they are extremely common! Plus, these things cannot be avoided. They are a part of life whether you're in a relationship or not, you will feel these things at some point in time. You're just making yourself nuts trying to avoid something you can't. Do you fear abandonment? Your partner probably does too, so communicate that. Do you feel vulnerable? Vulnerable means intimacy with the right person, it's genuine…it's unavoidable. Do you fear boredom? Spice it up with that person you have such a long-lasting connection with. You get where I'm going. It's that simple. Don't overthink it. Don't overcomplicate it, just attack it. I watch this show called Married at First Sight, which may be a bit cheesy to some of you but a doctor on the show said something very valuable I'd like to share with you: "Treat the problem in your marriage as the enemy. Not each other. Attack the problem because it's an enemy to your marriage." That's that partnership tactic. So, like the Nike ad says, "just do it!"

I guess some would say it's a good thing that we are holding off marriage because there's the decline of divorces that comes with that and they'd have a point. I just want marriages to last longer and be stronger. I think we should try harder, be more committed, honest, sympathetic, and smart. At the end of the day it's not about quantity it's about quality. Let's make it a normal thing to succeed in our relationships.

> "Genesis 2:18–25: "Then the LORD God said, 'It is not good that the man should be alone; I will make him a helper fit for him." –Anonymous

There really is a difference between a relationship and a partnership. Women should be striving for partnerships in our relationships. The reason why I was so hung up on the idea of partnership when I first heard of it was because nowadays, it's like women have to be the whole backbone and more in a relationship. Our culture has redefined what a woman is supposed to be. It seems we don't leave room for a partner and men don't want to be a partner anymore. They want to be a receiver, not a giver. Ladies, we talked about how we overcompensate for men and try to be the perfect wife, mom, coworker, and lover all at once. We concluded that it's impossible. We'll always fail at something if we are trying to do everything at once. So piggybacking off of that, let's talk about how you can't possibly go into a relationship alone! You need a partner. You're going to have a bad day, and a day you're slacking, so why not be with someone who understands that and can pick up for you?

"When we are expected to do everything at once, we fail because we are not focusing on that one thing we are supposed to be doing at that one time," a smart guy once told me. It's like you can be a jack of all trades, but you'll be master of none. Why are there so many roles attached to women nowadays anyway? Why do women take on all these roles and more? It's a whole topic that I just can't get into with

> ~~
> *"If you want to have a good partner, be a good partner."*
> *-Anonymous*
> ~~

one chapter, but my point in bringing it up now is to show you that women have this looming expectation over them to do everything well all the time, when we really need to expect to have a partner who can help us at any time!

Look, we don't live in days where women just stay home and be mommies and wives anymore. We live in a day where the demand for being a successful woman is much higher. It's amazing to be a woman nowadays, but it's also hard. Especially when men start to give us all their roles. It has become the norm and I say both genders are to blame. It's incredible that the less you need a partner, the more independent you're deemed to be. That's not always a positive…you must know how to work as a team, as I have told you before. Is he willing to help and are you willing to leave him space to help? God put women here to help the man, not do his job for him. Remember how we were created. So, it's time to start being with men who understand that we are human too, that we will have days when we look like poop, the kids are working on our nerves, the house isn't clean, laundry isn't folded, and dinner isn't cooked.

There will be days when we will need help! We have to be with men who will gladly lift that weight off of our shoulders when it's needed, and we have to be *willing to let them.* Is the guy you're with capable or even willing to do this? Are you? For quite some time I wasn't. I wasn't willing to let my husband help. I wanted to be a superwoman. I wanted him to need me for every little thing. That obviously became stressful. I had been seeing that independent woman role model my whole life and before I knew it, that's who I became. Then my husband had a real talk with me. It made it hard for him to do his job and, being the real man that he is, he wasn't having it. He straight up asked me, *how can I be a man if you won't let me?* That was a reality check.

I know a very successful woman with four kids, an amazing career as a doctor, and a successful marriage. She gave me a sound example concerning the point I am trying to make. Because of her advanced career and other duties, she could not continue to clean the house. Her husband helped by doing the house-cleaning for a while, but when he decided he couldn't anymore, they agreed to get a cleaner. Here's another example: Suppose one night you really don't feel like cooking. Is your man going to pick a fight with you because "that's what you're supposed to do", or is he going to try to make something for the household or order

"Partnerships are better than relationships because of this type of support, structure, give and take, and realistic approach."
-Perceptual Plazz

in? Do you see where I am going? That's a partnership. You solve problems together, not each treat the other as if they are the problem. I have an example that's close to home...when I lost my job. I was unemployed for a whole year due to the pandemic and that left all the weight of surviving on my husband. He understood, picked up extra shifts, and encouraged me that I was going to be alright. Never once did he complain, put me down, or threaten me. I considered myself "slacking". I applied for a variety of jobs, unemployment, and even started doing some freelance duties on the side to try to make up for my loss of income. I worked hard to be a great partner and so did my husband. You can bet that never once did he have to cook dinner, clean the house, or any of those kinds of things while he was carrying my financial weight. Partnerships are better than relationships because of this type of support, structure, give and take, and realistic approach to life. Because life is going to happen.

Let's summarize why partnerships are better than relationships:

1. There's healthy give-and-take in a partnership. if one partner is temporarily unable to carry his or her responsibility, the other one can pick up the weight. It's a team effort. It's just like kayaking or basketball.

2. Stability: It's like a contract. You're going to get wrinkles, your body is going to change, and your feelings may change some days, but what a partnership gives you through all change is stability. Something you can always count on!

3. Strength: Partnerships evolve with life to become stronger. Sometimes a bungee cord is better than a metal chain.

4. Partnerships last longer than relationships because relationships are founded on silly things like: looks, convenience (people who are scared to be alone and

both free, so they get in a relationship), and feelings: you see how I started this chapter? That's because some days you won't feel so good. The way feelings fluctuate could never give you a stable partnership but if you make a deal to support and always be there for one another no matter how you feel, you can't be stopped! That's what marriage is, it's a covenant.

5. Relationships are just a steppingstone. So why settle?

What is something that you could fix in your relationship to make it more like a partnership? What is something you could do to be more understanding, committed, and honest in your relationship?

_____

_____

_____

_____

_____

_____

_____

_____

_____

_____

_____

_____

_____

_____

_____

_____

_____

CHAPTER 8

Becoming Better Role Models

No one understands a woman like a woman. What we say and do to one another affects us on a whole different level. That's why it's important to be better role models to our young ladies. After all they are the future. So while this chapter might be a little awkward or funny, get the big takeaway: these icky conversations are necessary, maybe even vital! That means having all the icky conversations and setting an example by what you preach to your daughters. It's a big deal as I recall watching and taking in what my mother said and did as I grew up. My mom had a lot of icky talks with me that were necessary and that I am truly thankful for but there were still some things I wish I had known going into womanhood. Many of my girlfriends say the same thing. We already know being a woman in this day and

> ~~
> "Being A role model is the most powerful form of educating.
> -John Wooden"
> ~~

age is a bit different than when our grandmothers and mothers grew up, so therefore we should normalize having important conversations sooner with our loved ones. I'd even argue these things should be happening sooner nowadays. I'm talking about the meat and potatoes of womanhood: Sex, menstrual cycles, puberty, relationships, hygiene, and peer pressure! Those are big things in womanhood and they start at a very young age.

I'm coming out of the gate with the sex conversation. There are a few reasons why: 1) Young women are exposed to sex so much sooner nowadays. I know we are supposed to wait until marriage according to the Bible, but people are just not doing that. While I am a Christian I am also being realistic. 2) The molestation rate keeps climbing, and 3) so does the rate of single motherhood. But it all starts with that three-letter word that makes young girls a bit too curious...and you wanna know what the culprits are? Internet, music, friends, and even TV shows. Kids now just have access to so much information at their fingertips. And while you think you might have all the parental controls on your Netflix, Cable, and Wi-Fi, they still have access to things when they're out of your sight. Sex is one of those things and it's a big thing! A young lady should receive education about sex from their mom before anybody else. Health class or sexual education doesn't always do as much as you think it does. It's not always effective, and when you're surrounded by people your age it seems like it's a big joke. Or can be too much to handle. I just want to say the teachers don't emphasize the importance of certain things when it comes to sexual education. In fact, I don't really remember taking the class, that's how non-impactful it really was. So it would be better for both mom and daughter to sit down and have a conversation about sex, woman to young woman. Take that lecture out of the classroom and make it real by making it table talk with your daughter, it's needed! Tell your daughter sex should be shared with someone very important to her like fiancé or husband, and should always be safe until prepared for children. Sex isn't just physical, it's very emotional and spiritual. We have to be better at explaining the truth to our daughters about sex. That is something a sexual education course doesn't teach them. Explain the importance of a young woman losing her virginity, protection methods from pregnancy (like female condoms or other forms of birth control) and diseases that can result from not protecting ourselves properly or avoiding this conversation. Especially, there is also the emotional damage that comes from sex if not done correctly. Teach our young ladies there's a way to do sex.

Let's talk about the menstrual cycle and puberty! Those are huge for young ladies. I had a hard time with puberty. As you've learned about me, I had a lot of acne and tiny boobs and

~~

"Cover your Stump Before You Hump."

-Anonymous

~~

low self-esteem. These feelings and experiences are common for a lot of girls undergoing puberty. So it's possible your daughter feels the same or will feel the same. Imagine how impactful it would be if you told her you went through the same thing and how you got through it. We can't forget about the biggest part of puberty for a girl, the menstrual cycle. We shouldn't have to just learn about the basics of a period in

~~

"Proverbs 14:1: The wisest of women builds her house."

~~

health class. We need to learn how to cope with it and once again, that's something that class doesn't teach. Unlike some, I was lucky enough to start my period at home. However, when the time came for me to react, I didn't know what to do or why.

One day on the way to high school, I was sitting near the aisle on the bus as a popular girl walked up the steps. I will not mention her name because this is an embarrassing story. I remember her wearing these very short pink shorts. As she walked by me I smelled something foul, and then out of nowhere, I heard a PLOP! It sounded like something wet had hit the ground. When I looked down, I realized her soaked sanitary pad had fallen out of her shorts and onto the bus floor. She turned around and looked down as she realized her pad had fallen out of her shorts. She turned beet red, burst into tears, and ran off the bus with embarrassment. The bus driver had to put gloves on to pick it up and throw it away. The bus was full of cruel laughter and gossip the rest of the ride. She didn't come to school for the next two days. Can you imagine how embarrassing that is for a young lady? What advice would you give your daughter to avoid this? This is not a conversation the health class or sexual education teacher talks about. You see what I mean? A conversation about the different materials you could use for menstrual cycles: pads, tampons, or cups, etc. and proper attire you wear when you are on your period would have been ideal for this situation. I don't know, I just think it was messed up for her to learn that way!

Remember I told you I didn't know what to do when I got mine? Well, it was a weekend. I slept in and slowly tossed and turned until I decided to open my eyes. You know when you first get up you roll over to grab your phone? So I did. I felt something wet and sticky in between my legs. I put my fingers in my underwear and felt around. I looked at my hand which was covered in blood and freaked out. I jumped out of bed, flapped the covers open to see the whole bedspread looking something like a murder scene. I put on some new pants and underwear and ran to the bathroom. Now what happened after that ladies, is so embarrassing but hilarious. My mom had a habit of going to the grocery store in the morning when we were still asleep so I snuck into her room. In my household, going into mom's room when they aren't there or without permission is like asking for trouble, but I had no choice. At last, I found something—a tampon. I had learned about them in class and decided to wing it. Oh boy. I went into the bathroom, unwrapped the tampon, sat on the toilet, and pushed the thing up inside of me until I squirmed. I

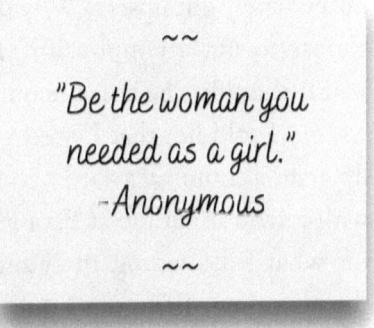

~ ~

"Be the woman you needed as a girl."
-Anonymous

~ ~

was still a virgin so it was more uncomfortable than I imagined it would be. I thought I had done good and went on about my day, uncomfortably. Later that afternoon, I was walking to my room, wiggling to keep the tampon from coming out, something I had been doing all day. It had been sliding up and down for hours and I preferred walking funny rather than putting my fingers up there and shoving it back up in front of people. So I walked like a newborn calf until I was behind closed doors.

My mom watched me silently then said, "Why are you walking like something's in your booty? What's wrong with you?" I pulled her into the bathroom and told her I had put a tampon in because I woke up to my period that morning. She immediately got upset. "Why didn't you call me? Why did you choose to put a tampon in?" I didn't know what to say. She said it shouldn't be that uncomfortable unless I did something wrong. I told her that I was in pain. Let me tell you my mom deserves a mommy award because she inspected me as she did with others at her job at Planned Parenthood. She explained to me what I did wrong and educated me on how to do it right the next time. Turns out I put the whole thing in, the tampon, and the applicator. I was supposed to use the applicator to push it in me and throw it away afterward. I didn't do that. Instead, I put the applicator and tampon in my vagina. No wonder it had been sliding in and out all day. It was very hard plastic! But think about how sexual education courses don't show you how to put tampons in or pads on? They don't tell you how often to change them and all the really important stuff. Imagine how beneficial it would have been for me and ol' girl with the tiny shorts, to learn these things ahead of time from our mommies.

> ~~
> "Children are great imitators so give them something great to imitate."
> -Anonymous
> ~~

The relationship talk is really big because even though you don't think about it much, your daughter is paying attention to you. So take accountability. The men that you have around her constantly, whether it's your boyfriend or your husband or just casual dates, have been picked up by your daughters. She has observed and when she's ready to date, she is most likely going to be going for the types of guys that she's used to being around her. It's only second nature. So it's important that moms lead by example; you can't tell her who she should be with and even get upset with her for making bad decisions in relationships if she observes you doing the same thing! You should set the pace and show her how it's done. Have a conversation with her about what her boyfriend should or shouldn't do, and prove it to her by acting it out in front of her. It's so important that moms talk to their daughters about guys.

Hygiene! When I was in my sophomore year of college, we had a girl on the track team and she was often gossiped about because her "downstairs department" often gave off a foul smell. It's moments like that I think about the importance of a mother having conversations about hygiene with her daughter. I won't get too icky but talk about how to properly wash your hoo-ha, not sitting on public toilets, not sleeping around, yeast infections, pH balance, and all the things ladies experience. Emphasize getting mammograms and pap smears and always making sure your young one is in good health. She'll thank you when she's older! My mother worked for Planned Parenthood so I had this conversation with my mother very often and although some of them were uncomfortable, I am so happy that I had them because if I have a daughter I will have the same conversations.

Peer pressure is something that doesn't really go away as you get older. Remember we talked about comparing? That's a form of peer pressure in adulthood. But when you're younger it's a lot more serious because you can be under peer pressure to do some very dangerous things. Things your friends are doing, the music tells you to do, or tv shows portray. Things like drinking alcohol, having sex, taking drugs, ditching class, and rebelling against the law. All those things can be very dangerous when they involve the young and uneducated. Not that breaking the law would be better at any age, but you catch my drift. For example, when I was sixteen I had a group of friends. They were all seniors and they often went to parties or hosted parties and I never was into it until they started pressuring me to go. I went to a party one night with college kids and high school seniors and they pressured me into drinking. I had never drunk alcohol before. Of course, as a first-timer, and as an uneducated person using alcohol, I overdid it. I passed out after throwing up several times and basically had alcohol poisoning! Think about how to address this with your daughters because the pressure of music, friends, and TV isn't going away. In fact, it's getting worse.

Let's stop waiting until it's too late to have these conversations. Choose the best time to talk about these things with your daughters. For some, fifteen may be too late while for others it may be too soon. However, whatever you do, make sure you have these conversations. Let's eliminate the embarrassment out of growing into a woman. Think about the stories I've shared and how they could have been avoided. They should have been.

What is something that you wish you knew before becoming a grown woman? How can you be a better role model for the younger ladies that look up to you?

_____

_____

_____

_____

_____

_____

_____

_____

_____

_____

_____

_____

_____

_____

_____

_____

_____

_____

CHAPTER 9

Stealing Fairytales, Stealing Men

We talked about divorces a chapter ago, now let's address the driving force behind many divorces — infidelity. Infidelity typically leads to break-ups. While we talked more about married couples, I am not leaving the unmarried folks out. You're still in the hot seat too. We all know both sexes cheat. Some would say men are more inclined to cheat. Others would say men just happen to be the ones who get caught while women are more sneaky about it. What truly matters is if the cheating person knows they are in a relationship and continues to cheat anyway! However, I feel the women who sleep with married men, really, really know better! While I am aware it takes two to cheat, and that the married man involved in an affair is even more guilty than the woman, I am just gearing this chapter towards the ladies messing with a married man. The homewreckers. Why do we wreck other women's dreams?

Why do women want other people's men? Do they see him as being worthy of their love? Do they think he would give them what he gives his significant other? Is it the compare, compete, and jealousy that we talked about in the previous chapters? Do women think single men are cursed? I thought yes to all those questions. This is just a theory, but maybe... just maybe women are attracted to these men because they see that he has those qualities every woman wants so it shows that he's an applicable candidate for themselves although he's off the market. Am I getting onto something with this? But who's to say that the single guy that keeps trying to take you on dates doesn't have those same qualities or isn't capable of having those qualities for you?

Okay while digging deep into this and hopping on Google to research the subject, I found something called the wedding ring effect. Have you ever heard of the wedding ring effect? It's defined as a woman being more romantically attracted to a man because he was good enough for someone else to take or marry. Apparently, something about it makes women want to jump on them even more. And they find themselves wishing and yearning for what someone else already has. I don't know how true it is, but it's interesting.

> ~~
> "A woman who walks in purpose doesn't have to chase people or opportunities. Her light causes people and opportunities to pursue her."
> - Dr. Farrah Gray
> ~~

Some of you may justify your actions by saying, "Well we aren't having sex, we just talk, hang out, and spend time together". However, you'd still be wrong because being a homewrecker isn't just about physically having intercourse with this taken man. It takes more than sex to be a homewrecker. Sending flirtatious text messages, meeting up, sneaking around for personal time WITHOUT the wife or girlfriend knowing, having deep conversations about what's going on in your lives, and confiding in each other about your relationships can all be cheating too. That is a different level of intimacy that should not be shared with people outside of the relationship. I think the non-physical things are even scarier than having sex because those are things that hold more meaning. Anyone can have sex but not everyone can have meaning. Sometimes that's the worst way to be a homewrecker.

We briefly discussed some trademarks which maker a homewrecker, but now it's essential to talk about why we should stop. When I say don't be a homewrecker, what I mean by that is to not implode or interrupt somebody else's home life and relationship all for yourself. Everyone has a right to love, but that isn't at the expense of someone else's family or marriage. What this chapter is aiming to do is talk to those of you who may be in love with somebody else's man. That makes you a homewrecker and you are just as much to blame as the man if you know he has a woman. I can't stress it enough that you need to back off. Some women have this bad feeling when they see a guy or have feelings for a guy that is married or taken, yet they still allow themselves to fall in love knowing that it's dead wrong. These women just put everyone else involved in the crossfire.

There is more than one reason why you should stop being a homewrecker. One is that you need to have respect for other people's lives. You don't know what they go through behind the scenes, you don't know their household, you don't know if there are children involved, or if their woman is crazy. Plus, both of you may be sneaking around and thinking that nobody will ever find out. That's a

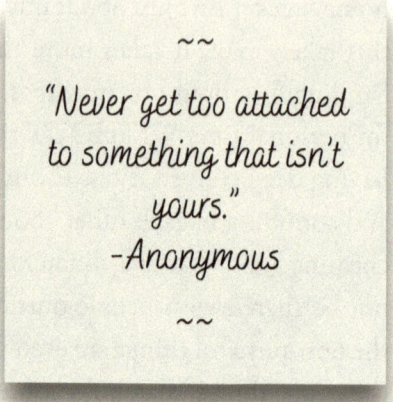

"Never get too attached to something that isn't yours."
-Anonymous

lie, everything comes to light eventually. Trust me she will find out and there's no telling her response when she does. If she's well-minded she'll just take it up with him because he's the one who knows he's in a relationship with her but if she's a little crazy she might come for you too. So why put yourself and your reputation in danger? You don't know what people will do for the love of their lives, sometimes there's nothing they won't do. Think about it, you wouldn't want someone to do that to you. The other reason is that he's with this woman for a reason! Unfortunately, I have been on the receiving end of infidelity. I was upset with the man but I couldn't help but find myself confused about why the woman would do that too. Another woman wrecked my home years ago. I'm sure some of you can relate. There is no justification whatsoever that could have fixed it. What hurt most is that the woman knew who I was and that we were together! The same way my boyfriend at the time did. Having my relationship disregarded and disrespected by another woman who just did not care that he was with me made me feel untrusting of other women, and only caused me to have serious trust issues. I felt betrayed by him the most but also by her as well. Women are reading this book right now who have been in my

~~

"The weakest thing a man could do is talk about his woman to another woman."
-Anonymous

~~

shoes and would probably agree that being in that situation sucks. When I hear about these stories I sometimes am just as upset with the woman who knows the wife or girlfriend as I am with the man. One lesson this situation taught me was to never be the other woman causing the chaos because it didn't feel good when it happened to me. It sucks to say but some of you won't learn that until it happens to you.

I try to look on the other side and see why a woman would put herself in this homewrecking predicament like I did earlier when we talked about a man who wouldn't put a title on it. This isn't much different - he doesn't have respect for you or his companion in both scenarios. So again, you have to have respect for yourself enough to walk away and respect for his wife. A real man wouldn't have an ongoing affair and string you and her along. He has cheated on his girlfriend or wife, what makes you think he wouldn't do that to you? My momma always said, "You lose men, how you get them." Just because you get involved doesn't mean he's going to leave her. It's selfish and naive for you to expect him to. It's also not a good place for you to put yourself.

So don't put yourself in a position where you are always second and being hurt. I know we all

> *"If a relationship has to be a secret, you shouldn't be in it."*
> *- Regina Brett*

want a Princess Tiana and Cinderella fairytale. I think the reason women become homewreckers is the desire to be loved like everyone else. There's nothing wrong with wanting to be loved, it's what you do to get it that can be righteous or disastrous. At first, it may seem like a fairytale; flirtatious, finishing each other's sentences, going on dates, all the exciting stuff, all the good stuff...but affairs are always messy and painful and they never have a happy ending. The truth is you deserve more. You deserve your own full-time companionship with your man who you don't have to share or try to steal from anyone else. You are not meant to be someone's side chick! Don't you want more? Aren't you worth more?

Big Takeaways

1. You deserve love too, but not at the wife's, husband's, and your own expense.

2. If you're sleeping with a married man…honey, you are just as guilty!

3. The man isn't going to treat you well if he doesn't treat his wife well.

4. It's not just about having sex, there are other ways to cheat. If you have to hide it, you probably shouldn't be doing it.

5. Women, we all want the same things—a fairytale. We should build our sisterhood and respect each other.

Have you experienced or participated in infidelity, if so what did you learn? How did this chapter make you think about your relationship?

_____

_____

_____

_____

_____

_____

_____

_____

_____

_____

_____

_____

_____

_____

_____

_____

_____

_____

CHAPTER 10

Choose You, Don't Lose You

"Don't lose yourself. Now that you're married, and when you become a mom...just whatever you do, don't lose yourself," an associate said to me. It had me thinking about how women in long-term relationships just give up themselves.

I've seen glimpses of it in my five-year relationship. I don't get my hair done as much, wear make-up as much, do as many things I enjoyed, you catch my drift. One day it hit me that if I noticed, he had to notice, right?

> "Taking care of yourself is the pathway to fulfillment and to high performance in work and in life. And, just as importantly, it's a gift to others."
> –Brene Brown

Doesn't it just mean I'm comfortable? Is it his responsibility to notice? Isn't he the person I do these things for?

While relationships are key components (later we'll unravel why that is) where women lose themselves, so is motherhood, careers, and even where they are in life. Yeah, sure it's great you can be real with your husband and kids but you have to be real with yourself—you've let yourself and what you love go. And I know when you get married you unite but remember how to coexist. I think it doesn't help that marriage is seen as the main event of a woman's life because once she has it, she settles. Happiness should be our main event! Things you love don't have to be sacrificed just because you have a family. I get it— the juggling of changing diapers, feeding the kids, seducing your husband in the bedroom, and being a CEO at work, can easily loosen the grip you have on yourself and what you enjoy doing. That doesn't mean it should be acceptable though. Some blame it on being too busy, broke, depressed, stressed, tired, while others are comfortable, want out of their relationship, or are just plain lazy. The saddest excuse I've seen for women losing themselves is their partner doesn't like them to do the things that make them happy. In other words, the women's hobbies become a conflict in the relationship.

> ~~
> *"By tossing away our own passions and interests, women lose their authenticity."*
> *-Vicky Larson*
> ~~

If your partner and what makes you happy are in conflict, you need to do some re-evaluating because you deserve to be happy and no loved one should ever hold you back from your happiness. I have been there and done that. I had an ex-boyfriend who used to get jealous about karaoke nights and girl dates. He purposely tried to keep me home and we got into a fight every time I wanted to go out with friends without him. That's toxic.

I read this article published by the HuffPost titled *Why Do Women Lose Themselves in Marriage?* And it really got me thinking. The article led me to a book which then led me to this quote,"She'll pretend to agree when she doesn't really agree, she'll go along with things she doesn't really believe in, and if she does that long enough, she'll no longer know what she feels," Author Beverly Engel states in one of her books, "There can be no truly happy outcome to that." No matter how successful, assertive, or powerful some women are, the moment they become involved with a man they begin to give up part of themselves—their social life, their time alone, their spiritual practice, their beliefs and values," Engel writes. "In time, these women find they have merged their lives with their partners' to the point where they have no life to go back to when and if the relationship ends." FACTS! Isn't that scary?

I have a real-life example: When I was in college I had a very intelligent friend. She aimed to put off dating until she met the right guy at the right time, which meant outside of college to her. In the meantime, she was busy leading organizations, being an athlete, and making the dean's list every semester. She was also the most Christian college student I knew. Soon enough she started dating this guy. Immediately she started to behave differently. Things she said she shouldn't do or wouldn't do became her habits! She stopped doing things she enjoyed doing and started doing things that he liked to do. She started to party, drink, be late to class, and curse - all things completely out of her character. And I realized there was a true problem when it came to her Christianity. Her boyfriend was not a believer in God, and she was. I started to see her take less part in church, less part in Christian activities like reading the Bible, leading prayer nights, and going to Bible studies, and before she knew it she hadn't gone to church in months! I saw her go from not even having social media profiles to posting every day on different platforms. She made all these changes and eventually lost touch with what she enjoyed doing, ultimately her true self. There are so many examples of women shifting and losing who they are because they are in a relationship. This one was crazy to see in person though.

I've seen it time and time again where women become less happy and enjoyable because they stop doing the things they enjoy. They've given up their hobbies, friendships, settled in, stopped "prettying up", stopped cooking and cleaning, all just to keep their relationship. They just seem to stop caring and being happy. And the lack of happiness will affect you and all of your relationships with your husband, kids, coworkers, and relatives. We stop doing the little things we like. We have to do things for ourselves too! We make everything about our men but what we enjoy shouldn't be something we do for him! He could probably care less, especially if he is still doing things he enjoys. So we know it exists but what do we do about it?

You can start by not forgetting the positives of who you are or were before you merged with your man and became a mom to your children. Remember who you used to be? Before your boyfriend, fiancé, husband, or children? I'm not talking about the negative parts of you that needed

~~

"At times it seems we should trade selflessness for a bit of selfishness."
-Perceptual Plazz

~~

to change, I'm talking about the part of you that you actually enjoyed! The parts of you who did things that made you happy and made you...you. The woman your man fell in love with and the woman you were in love with. Which is a happier one. Remember to always love the things that you love. If you love to do poetry, make sure you go to poetry nights at your favorite lounge, if you love to go get your nails done, go get your nails done, practice individuality even though you're in a serious relationship, even though you're a mom. Don't lose yourself in everything that everybody else wants and needs. Don't make your whole life all about them. Make sure that you're still having fun, following your dreams, and being your own person. Stop sacrificing your individuality!

At times it seems we should trade selflessness for a bit of selfishness. After all, this is a self-help book, you picked it up for yourself! You have to know when to put yourself first because your happiness matters too. Lose weight, eat right, get pretty but do it for you! It's time to get back to the things that you enjoy. Going out with your girls, painting, dancing, singing, reading, exercising, etc. You need to rest, you need to laugh, you need to be free—you need to be happy. Tell your hubby, kids, and boss you are taking a personal leave day! Do it so you can take care of yourself. Even if that personal emergency day is having a lazy day, going to a painting class, or meeting your girlfriends for a long picnic. Do it.

A little selfishness is good for you sometimes. Practice doing these things now so you can be better in the long run. You know when you're on the plane and they say "put your mask on before you help others." Same concept! You can only make sure to fulfill your happiness. Part of being a good wife, a good mother, friend, or relative is taking care of yourself. You can't do that if you are unhappy. Focus on you because truly the only thing you can control is you and your life. So make sure while you are taking care of everything else and everyone else you don't forget about yourself. Choose you, don't lose you!

Things to enforce and start practicing

1. Spend at least an hour every day doing something you love.

2. Book a massage or a nail day every month.

3. Set up a girls picnic or night out every month.

4. Put the kids to bed early at least one day out of the week to spend time with your husband, ALONE.

5. Don't feel bad or let anybody shame you for putting yourself first sometimes.

How can you get back to doing things you love, that happier place? Have you lost touch with the old, happier you? Have you forgotten what you enjoy because you're too busy making everyone else happy?

_____

_____

_____

_____

_____

_____

_____

_____

_____

_____

_____

_____

_____

_____

_____

_____

_____

_____

CHAPTER 11

Watch Your Company

I call it hating but there's a good ole' saying that goes, misery loves company. Google says: ***Misery loves company means people who are suffering are comforted by the knowledge that others are also unhappy.*** Have you ever had some good news to tell someone and you just see the hate on their face or hear the hate in their voices when you share your news? They don't seem all too excited or happy for you. These miserable people will always find a reason to laugh and belittle your achievements and sometimes they are closer to you than you'd like to admit.

The only reason why they behave that way is because of jealousy or misery. Imagine that hating person being someone you consider a good friend or even a family member. It can even be your significant other trying to hold you back. It happens. It is much more common than you think. We already talked about jealousy but this, this is tougher. It hits so much harder when it's someone close to you that is trying to silently sabotage your life. I've been through it several times. It always seems the higher you climb in life, there are always people trying to pull you down—just like monkeys in a barrel.

I have been so hurt by the people I call family and close friends because they weren't content with themselves. Because they wanted to be like me or better than me. Or just

"Real situations always expose fake people. Pay attention"
-Trent Shelton

because they weren't happy with something going on in their lives. It got weirder for me when my ex-boyfriend was jealous of me. Here's a story: I had a boyfriend in junior college who was on the men's track and field team. He was fast. So fast he was considered to be one of the fastest sprinters on the track team. I was considered to be one of the fastest on the women's track team. We were a perfect pair, it seemed. So while it started like the movie Love and Basketball, it soon got a little too competitive. He would be condescending in his remarks about my races when he won his. He would be silent at times that I deserved congratulations all because he didn't do well in his races. He would belittle my accomplishments because he didn't accomplish the same things or more. However, his jealousy and negative company really smacked me in the face when we started to receive offer letters for track and field scholarships to go to the university level. He counted every letter that came in, mine and his. He compared our letters and got upset when I received more letters and higher offers than he did. Eventually, I had to stop telling him when I received offers and even stop letting him read them. Every little thing became a competition and not the good kind. But it wasn't just him. I started to notice people I grew up with acting funny as well. I got the same responses from them that I had gotten from the jealous boyfriend. Your friends and family aren't always on your side. What a shocker right? (Extreme sarcasm). I suck at sarcasm, I know. Anyway, they'd say mean things like: That's not even a good university; You shouldn't go there because those girls are so much faster than you; You'll never win anything; Girl, they are trying to get any athlete they can; Don't feel special.

That's not all. I have an example I have seen many people go through. How many times have you noticed a person you called a friend talk behind your back, tell your

> ~~
>
> *"Handle your business without people knowing your business."*
> *-Anonymous*
>
> ~~

business, and start acting distant? Then we're surprised when that same so-called friend is laid up with your boyfriend, who is now your ex because you found out they were sneaking around together? This is the same friend you called and talked about your relationship problems with too. Have you ever heard the song My Man by Tamar Braxton? It's a tearful song about the betrayal of her man who cheated on her with her friend! While she spends a great deal addressing her man, as she should, she addresses both of them. It goes a little something like this:

"Never trust a lonely woman with the one you love

She ate dinner at my table, even watched my kids

And she took my man...

She called me about her man, but I didn't understand

She was talking 'bout my man..."

It gets back to that homewrecker conversation we had only this time, I'm telling you to watch who you're surrounded by.

> ~~
>
> *"I think it's important to get surroundings as well as yourself into a positive state - meaning surround yourself with positive people, not the kind who are negative and jealous of every little thing you do."*
> *-Heidi Klum*
>
> ~~

Anyway, continuing with my story, after being upset by all the shade people were throwing at me, one day it just hit me: *It isn't my job to make people feel secure in their lives. Their jealousy isn't about me at all. It isn't my job to make people happy for me. Why do I even care? I should keep striving to be successful if that's what I want to do. Why should I keep these people around me?*

Why did I expect every person in my circle to be just as happy for me as I was for myself? Why did I feel the need to get their validation on my life decisions? Why did I look for their approval? How come when I was on the same level as them, they didn't behave this way?

I never understood why people got jealous of others doing better than them. Especially when the person worked their butt off to get there. I mean odds are you don't know what that person went through. I faced many adversities and obstacles to get to where I am today. And for the same people that cheered for me in the bleachers during my biggest track meets to become my enemies was a tough pill to swallow. However, part of being human is being imperfect. There isn't always logic to the things we do or say. Jealousy and misery can make you do things you would never do if you were in your right mind. I forgave these people. That doesn't mean that I became naive and surrounded myself with those types of people though. I decided to do the exact opposite. I still have no choice but to talk to a number of those people today but it doesn't mean that I don't side-eye them sometimes or watch what I say around them. It doesn't mean I tell them all my business and set myself up to feel that way again. Why? Because they are haters. They are sippin' on hater-ade…that's why.

I read this quote years ago and it's stuck with me ever since: "Take the knife they put in your back out and use it to cut the ropes." I don't remember where I read it or heard it but it struck a chord with me. Now, I am very selective about who I surround myself with.

~~

"If people are doubting how far you can go, go so far you can't hear them anymore."
-Michele Ruiz

~~

It doesn't matter to me if you're a friend, boyfriend, or family member. The fact of the matter is someone who claims to love you should never wish harm on you and want you to hurt or fail. They're supposed to build you, not break you. They should want the best for you, not celebrate silently when you fail. They should always be trustworthy and want you to be happy. If they are everything but these things, they are full of nonsense because you should never treat a person you love harshly or enviously.

The problem is we are afraid to lose these bad people. We are afraid to tell them like it is. We are afraid to tell them they are bad for our mental and emotional health and our lives. There is literally no legitimate reason to carry around dead weight and that's what bad people are…dead weight. Cut them off. Sometimes you have to love people from far away. I want to call out the quote you see on the previous page, and to add this one: "If people are doubting how far you can go, go so far you can't hear them anymore," said by Michele Ruiz. Instead, you should be bonding with people who have the same goals as you and mentality as you. If you mention you are trying to do something or no longer want to do something to improve your life, they should be happy for you and HELP, not deplete, belittle, or try to derail your plan. Definitely not on purpose… pick up on the signs. If you end up noticing them, back off. They don't need to know your every move. Hustle in silence. The same way you watch your figure, watch your favorite T.V. shows and watch your kids, you should be watching your company. The people in your circle can make you or break you if you let them!

<u>Big Takeaways</u>

1. Be careful what you tell people about your personal life.

2. Be vigilant about the negative, miserable, people around you who always have something negative to say...even about the most positive things.

3. Be happy for your loved ones and friends.

4. Celebrate with the people you love, don't be a hater or a jealous person.

What can you do to keep your peace no matter who is around you? What did you learn about yourself and your surroundings from this chapter?

_____

_____

_____

_____

_____

_____

_____

_____

_____

_____

_____

_____

_____

_____

_____

_____

_____

_____

CHAPTER 12

That's it! That's all!

I've got some exciting news... I'm pregnant! What a way to wrap up this book huh? About chapter 9, I found out that I was expecting and this book became all the more real to me. So I couldn't end this book without talking about pregnancy, another check mark added to my womanhood and sisterhood.

How did I find out you might ask? I went to do my yearly check-up, you know—Pap smear, STI tests and while they were at it they did a pregnancy test. The doctor came in and said that I tested positive for one of the tests. My heart fell into my stomach because she ran so many different tests and I was immediately concerned. She read the look on my face and smiled. She said, "Don't worry you don't

> ~~
>
> "Stay positive. The only difference between a good day and a bad day is your attitude."
> Anonymous
>
> ~~

have aids, or syphilis, or anything and your Pap smear looks great...but you're pregnant!"

I paused because I didn't think I heard correctly. And I said "What?! Did you grab the right urine cup?" I laughed hard and then I called my husband and told him the news with tears in my eyes—what a day!

Immediately I started to think about all the things that made me ready to be a mom and some things that I would have to adjust to before becoming a mom. Not that the adjusting would stop as I was "mommying". But being pregnant has a way of making you think about being a better person. Being as great as you can possibly be for this little blob growing in your womb that somehow already has a heartbeat. Someone you haven't even met! Being pregnant has made me different, and I'm not just talking physically, but emotionally, and mentally too. Being pregnant has taught me to be patient, flexible, dependable, to take care of myself, etc. It was so much more than the topical stuff, getting enough sleep, eating right, planning the near future. It was about adding more to my womanhood, becoming a better woman.

Creating a human is nothing short of a miracle. Although it may be uncomfortable, gross, painful, lonely, and embarrassing at times, it's been one of the most beautiful experiences of my entire life. To look in the mirror and say I created a person and even have the capacity to do it, makes my life more worth living and it's something I CHOSE to be positive about. Pregnancy to some women is a negative thing.... Everyone has different expectations and experiences. However, I want you to follow along here to see where I am going with this. Being happy about something and continuing to get better is a choice.

That's why I told people much later in my pregnancy that I was expecting—I am talking six and a half months and some didn't find out until the baby shower at 33 weeks. I didn't want any of their negative stories, opinions, expectations, or distractions to deter my mentality. I kept myself off of Google and any of those mommy blogs or groups and I only talked to people I really trusted and felt were positive. If you are anything like me you take things too personal, lose sleep, and overthink. I surrounded myself with positivity and I felt much better about pregnancy. I actually enjoyed my pregnancy because of this! I think my life will be better because of what I have learned in my pregnancy and even writing this book, which confirmed so many things for me. I think we can take this same approach I used during my pregnancy into being a better woman in general.

And now I laugh at all the funny things that have happened. I've peed myself at least ten times when sneezing, threw up tea and pork chops, got kicked in the ribs and pubic bone, have nagging backaches and gas, and the list goes on. Pregnancy has reminded me of

> ~~
>
> *"Rejoice always, pray without ceasing, give thanks in all circumstances; for this is the will of God in Christ Jesus for you."*
> *1 Thessalonians 5:16-18*
>
> ~~

life, you never know what to expect. You just roll with the kicks and punches. You wing it! As a woman, we never really know what's going to be a challenge for us in our lives. Although we discussed the things that hit most women, there will be more. You just gotta go with it.

Pregnancy has reminded me that we continue to add checkmarks to our womanhood and sisterhood as we keep living. And even Chapter 8 about Becoming Better Role Models hit me in the face. I now have to be a great role model as I found out I am having a girl. All these conversations I've had with you here, I can't wait to have with my daughter. Another woman who will pave the way for others and experience the things I have. And somehow we're all still so connected. We're SISTERS FOR LIFE. Remember what you wrote in this book, what you learned about yourself, and the decisions you tend to make in life. Remember the teachings of God and the funny-but-real quotes featured in this book that drove the point home. I guarantee there will be a time you'll need to reflect on something in between these pages.

Here's one more numbered list:

1. Remember why you picked up this book. Something in your life wasn't working and you sought change.

2. Now that we have digressed about most parts of being a woman, it's up to you to make the changes. You know what you receive is what you put in.

3. Change your life because you have the strength to do so.... God made you a woman and women are

incredible. We have the potential to be and do anything we put our minds to.

4. Remember you'll keep adding checkmarks to your womanhood and sisterhood. Don't get lazy and don't stop working.

5. Remember to keep it real with yourself.

6. Choose to be positive and choose to be better.

I've left you one more checklist—your self-evaluation quiz and don't worry if you can't check all these off now. You can always come back. Plus the story never ends and the progress never should stop. I want you to take what you've learned about yourself and other women with you. This is a never-ending journey. Complete your last journaling and the checklist with this question in mind, do you remember why you picked up this book?

Do you remember why you picked up this book? What has changed since you started it? Is there something you could continue to work on?

_____

_____

_____

_____

_____

_____

_____

_____

_____

_____

_____

_____

_____

_____

_____

_____

_____

_____

_____

_____

Self-evaluation Quiz

- You have learned how to put yourself first when needed
- Your emotions no longer control your life
- You can see a change taking place in your life
- You no longer feel bad about yourself
- You know how to be a better friend and companion
- You no longer deny who you are
- You no longer feel the need to compare yourself to other women
- Forget it…mark ALL THE ABOVE!

www.ingramcontent.com/pod-product-compliance
Lightning Source LLC
Chambersburg PA
CBHW031413120626
46545CB00006B/2130